Congress-led Coalition Government

Congress-led Coalition Government

Crisis to Crisis 2009 – 2011

C.P. Bhambhri

SHIPRA

₹ 650; US$ 32.50

ISBN: 978-81-7541-624-6

First Published in India in 2012

Congress-led Coalition Government: Crisis to Crisis—2009-2011

Published by:
SHIPRA PUBLICATIONS
H.O.: LG 18-19, Pankaj Central Market, Patparganj,
I.P. Ext., Delhi-110092, Tel: 91-11-2223 5152, 2223 6152
Br.Off.: 4617/18, Ansari Road, Darya Ganj,
New Delhi-110002, Tel: 6594 6453, 9810522367
E-mail: info@shiprapublications.com
www.shiprapublications.com

Preface

The central government, led by the Congress-led United Progressive Alliance, has failed to show any capacity to lead the country from 2009 to 2011. Its performance in the domestic and foreign policy spheres has been quite 'status quoist' because it has not shown any innovativeness or initiative in grappling with the challenges in any policy area. The government has been reactive and passive. The story is told in this study. An attempt has been made to analyse and explain the record of the government on the basis of facts and arguments. Thanks are due to D Kumar of Shipra Publications and Kuldeep Kumar of the JNU Office of Distinguished Scholar.

C.P. Bhambhri

Contents

Section II

Foreign Policy

Introduction

Who Rules Us: Bourgeois social science theory has always concerned itself primarily with the investigation of 'visible' and 'observable' faces of party leaders – the political executive and professional bureaucrats are seen to be responsible for policy making. Social scientific theory, primarily devoted to the analysis of only the 'observable' social facts, is quite inadequate in finding explanations for the complex reality of governance. The primary reason for its inadequacy is that it concentrates on the visible shadow of reality at the cost of exploring 'substance', which lies behind and beyond the so-called concrete governing classes, either political or bureaucratic.

Politics is embedded in history, economy, society and culture, and is not insulated from social forces at work beyond the territorial boundaries of a nation-state. How does industrialist Anil Ambani of Reliance ADAG get appointments with key officers of the Prime Minister's Office every Wednesday? Why are retired executives of public sector undertakings and IAS officers employed on lucrative terms by private industrial houses? One illustration may be given to substantiate the argument that state/politics and capital (big industrial and business firms) are intimately connected and involved in 'joint public policy making'. Former Steel Authority of India Ltd Chairman SK Rungta joined Anil Agarwal's Vedanta Aluminum Ltd as managing director. A comment will clarify the argument that the distinction between the state, elected political representatives, professional bureaucrats and the exploiting ruling and oppressing classes is non-existent. 'While serving senior executives may still be difficult to find, retired PSU chiefs are a big draw. While the private sector gets access to the goodwill and understanding of the bureaucracy that PSU retirees bring to the table, corporate governance experts warn of a potential conflict of interests.' Can capital be classified as public and private, or state and private entrepreneurship? The practitioners of bourgeois social science cannot distinguish between wood and trees because their theory does not equip them to find the real meaning of social facts and concrete reality. Here Marxist scientific social theory intervenes by focusing attention on the material, productive system of the social structure, which determines social, political and cultural relations in society.

Eric Hobsbawm has elaborated the Marxist theory of state and politics by focusing attention on its evolution from the 1840s to the later stages of Marxist theoretical sophistication. He states that 'the early communist form of Marx's theory of the state' had suggested that 'the essence of the state was political power', an expression of the opposition of classes within bourgeois society, and 'the present system it represented not a general interest of society but the interest of the ruling class (es).'[1] Such an early theorization of the essence of the state is more enlightening for the analysis of the political complexity of India than the liberal democratic theory of the western capitalist societies, beginning from John Locke to John Stuart Mill to John Rawls. The role of politics is central in Marxist theory, however, politics does not hang in the air or functions in a social vacuum, and capitalist society gets divided into 'classes' and if politics of the ruling classes is to control the state in its own service for accumulation of social surplus, the politics of the oppressed, suppressed and exploited 'basic underclasses' is to launch struggles to 'secure itself against its own representatives and officials', in order to avoid 'the transformation of the state and state organs from servants of society into its masters.'[2] To sum up this discussion, bourgeois theorists only see shadows, just the tip of the iceberg of politics, Marxists catch the bull by its horn because for them politics through class struggle is a prime mover of society for the replacement and displacement of the ruling class(es) from the corridors of state power.

The Indian political and social reality deserves mention for the purpose of explaining the complex and contradictory social forces and processes at work in the country?

First, the Indian capitalist state, fully supported by every fraction of domestic capitalist classes, has integrated itself with global capitalist system, led by crisis-ridden centres of finance-capital like the United States and European Union. This integrated global capitalist system has further blurred the distinction between the foreign and domestic politics of different societies. India is not only providing hospitality to foreign direct investment and joint ventures of developed capitalist countries, the big industrial houses of India led by the Tatas, Ambanis, Birlas, Mittals *et al.* are also investing in the US, the UK, Africa, West Asia, East Asia, etc. The capitalist state of India is acting as a midwife of foreign investors and also as an agent of big industrialists who have become global players.

Second, the capitalist path of development followed by India has generated social inequalities among classes and regions, and sharpened rural-urban divisions. While India was always a heterogeneous society, social divisions have become accentuated because of the way the capitalist state has operated its agenda of nation-building.

Third, causes of the rising inequality lie in the role of politics and political formations representing diverse fractions and strata of the bourgeoisie.

Marx always insisted that the working classes should have their own political party to further class struggle. Political parties of the working classes have become marginal because the oppressed perceive themselves in terms of caste, sub-caste, region, religion, etc and the consequence of all these social factors is that India's working classes have not been able to launch a large-scale mass struggle against either Indian capitalism or its mentors, the western headquarters of finance capital.

If politics is the site of action, the space is available to both capitalists and labour in a parliamentary competitive multipolar party democracy. The social class struggle of India is complex and it encompasses the big bourgeoisie, who are also global operators; middle/regional bourgeoisie, who operate in their specific regions and are supported by regional political formations; and entrepreneurial classes such as professionals, financiers, bankers and real estate operators, who are an important fraction of the bourgeoisie but with interests slightly different from the big bourgeoisie. The upper-middle and lower-middle classes are the 'moneyed' classes, and they can identify themselves with either the working-class movements and parties or with socially conservative exploiting classes and their political formations. The whole hierarchy of middle classes functions around the goals and values of social security and the social status quo. Ritualized religiosity is practised by the anxiety-ridden and insecure strata of the middle classes, who provide a solid social base to the communal-fascist Sangh Parivar and its political face, the BJP.

It is not without reason that the modern professional upper-middle classes, along with other fractions of middle- and lower-middle classes, wish to get all benefits from the capitalist path of development and also at the same time regularly visit modern temples like Delhi's Akshardham, built in the 1990s. This India co-exists very uncomfortably with more than 500 million unskilled, uneducated people, described as 'below poverty line'.

How does one substantiate the argument that the interests of fractions of classes are promoted and protected by political parties, whether all-India or regional? How does one explain that the 'unequal democracy' of India is operated and controlled by parties representing the interests of fractions of classes? The American National Association of Manufacturers stated: 'We have been in New York since before the turn of the century (20th century), because we regarded this city as the centre of business and industry. But the thing that affects business most today is government. The interrelationship of business with business is no longer so important as the interrelationship of business with government. In the last several years that has become very important.[3] Hence we have shifted to Washington DC.' India is no exception to this general rule and associations of industrialists are located in Delhi and capitalists of every state continuously keep influencing and lobbying governmental decision-makers to promote and protect the interests of industrialists.

The telecommunication industry has been taken over completely by predatory capitalists with the full connivance and sanction of the political executive of the central government. Pranab Mukerjee, while addressing a joint meeting of CEOs of FICCI-CII and Associated Chambers of Commerce and Industry on March 1, 2011 asked, 'I request your support to build consensus. Not only for the constitutional amendments for the Goods and Services Tax, the concurrence of state is essential. If the parties agree, I can get the Bills passed in this session (of Parliament).' He further stated, 'I seek your (India Inc's) support ... as you have influence over state governments you have interactions across the political spectrum of the country'.[4] Do we need any more evidence to substantiate the argument that capital and the state in India have been completely integrated and the state is actively promoting the interests of private capital?

In an article 'Indian Development Trumps (OR TURNS?) Dysfunctional', Jim Yardley observes 'India is richer than ever, with rising Gilded influence. Yet its development is divisive at home. It is experiencing a Golden Age of nouveau rich billionaires while it is cleaved by inequality and plagued in some states by poverty and malnutrition levels rivaling those of sub-Saharan Africa. The volatile contradictions ricochet daily through Indian life'.[5]

Public data based on official documents lead one to conclude that disparities and social inequalities have deepened in India and the responses of the state are piecemeal because people cannot be ignored in any parliamentary democratic system where elections are held at regular intervals. If Pranab Mukerjee is openly seeking the support of big industrial houses for public policies, the political executive of such a state is essentially exploiting pro-classes and very marginally it is pro-poor or pro-'basic classes'. The picture becomes clear when the operations of capitalists like the Ambanis or the Tatas are brought out in the open. Hamish McDonald observes: 'Again, Dhirubhai was not unique in cultivating officials. Many companies had their friends in the bureaucracy. Business like to get close to power and officials looked to post-retirement jobs or opportunities for their children.'[6] This led Sunil Bharti Mittal, the chairman of the Bharti group, to observe: 'The government and Mittal industry are working together on forming a coalition to address it', the mutual problems.'[7] The above narrative clearly proves that neo-liberalism, which is a 'project of class hegemony', can face comfortable serious 'crisis situations' by controlling the managers of the state.

Why is the working class not able to challenge class hegemony and the class state? Why is the Left, representing the working class interests, marginalised and proving incapable of exploiting the social crisis situation created by neo-liberal economic polices pursued by India?[8] How is such inequality in absolute terms persisting without a real working class challenge? The Forbes list of world billionaires for 2011 mentions 55 Indian billionaires in 2011, up from 49 in 2010, and it goes on to state further that 'India with its 55 billionaires has the third largest pool of billionaires, after the US and China.[9] A central question that deserves an answer is: Why is the exploitative and oppressive rule by the capitalist state and the exploiting ruling classes not faced with any strong challenge and resistance from the exploited labouring classes of India?

A biographer of Marx, Francies Wheen, says that for Marx 'social consciousness was the fertilizer for revolution'.[10] The crux of the issue is that the exploitative social, economic system is continuing because the labouring classes have not developed a level of social consciousness that can lead them to launch struggles against social oppressors. The social dialectics of India have revealed very contradictory trends. First, universal adult franchise and the competitive party and electoral system have shaken the foundations of the inherited hierarchical, caste and religiously dominated social structure. The urban and rural labouring classes have become conscious of their rights in a bourgeois democracy. India has experienced many social assertions and struggles launched by the marginal strata and socially excluded and deprived strata of society. The lower-middle classes, landless agricultural workers, marginal farmers, and other deprived strata of urban and rural society have become quite 'demanding' in return for their precious right to vote. Electoral battles have become highly competitive and the ordinary 'voter' has come to occupy centre stage in the country's democratic processes. This is the positive side of the social dialectics and the political level of social consciousness of Indian voters has reached a state where the 'demands' of the poor are taken note of by political parties of every fraction and strata of the ruling classes, whether all-India or regional. 'If social consciousness is the fertilizer' of social revolution, Indians have not achieved that level of social consciousness where they can unitedly, on the basis of common social struggles, pose a real threat to the domination of the ruling classes and political executive of the state.

The ironical situation in India is that transformation in the levels of social consciousness is held hostage to inherited social categories of the pre-capitalist past like caste- and priestly class-dominated religiosity. The Indian bourgeoisie is not a patron-in-chief of a modern scientific and secular society; on the contrary, they openly patronise superstition and ritual-based religiousity among the masses and industrial and commercial classes, including modern professional entrepreneurial upwardly mobile middle classes, and extend 'full support' to the communal-fascist Sangh Parivar of the Hindu rashtravadis. The BJP, a political mask of the exclusivist Hindu joint family of the Sangh Parivar, has been legitimised by the big to medium business classes, irrespective of the fact that the Parivar practises divisive politics. It is not only religion-based political and social divisions that have helped in the fragmentation of social consciousness of the Indian masses, the caste system, a relic of the past, has continued to play havoc in society and working class consciousness has been splintered into sub-ideologies. Hence the social soil is quite fertile for the continuance of rule by the exploiting classes.

Notes

1. Eric Hobsbawam, How to Change the World , *Tales of Marx and Marxism 1840-2011*, UK, Little Brown, 2011, p. 52.
2. Quoted by Hobsbawam, p. 57.
3. *Politics and Society*, Vol. 38, Number 2, June 2010, quoted by Hcker and Pierson, p. 176.

4. *Indian Express,* New Delhi, March 2, 2011, p. 1.
5. Jim Yardley, *The New York Times* (in the *Asian Age*-New Delhi) July 2, 2011, p. 2.
6. Manish McDonlad, *Ambani and Sons: The Making of the World's Richest Brothers and their Feud,* New Delhi, Lotus Collection, Roli Books, 2010, p. 88.
7. *The Economic Times,* New Delhi, August 2, 2011, p. 13.
8. Also Leo Panitch, Greg Albo and Vivek Chibber, (Eds.) *Socialist Register,* 2011 *The Crisis This Time,* New Delhi, Leftword Books, 2010, p. 323.
9. *The Hindustan Times,* New Delhi, March 10, 2011, p. 25.
10. Francies Wheen, *Max's Das Capital: A Biogrpahy,* Bhopal, Manjul Publishing House Pvt. Ltd., 2009.

Section I
Nation and States Politics

Not Just a Question of Rhetoric

The Congress party has come to occupy the leading position within the UPA coalition government at the Centre. Unlike the 14th Lok Sabha where the Congress had only 156 seats of its own, it has emerged as the centre of power in the 15th Lok Sabha with 206 seats of its own in the House of 543. It deserves to be underlined that the pro-*aam-aadmi* (comman man) agenda of the Congress is not based on any rhetoric. As Sonia Gandhi stated at the meeting of the Congress Parliamentary Party, the voters of India have renewed their confidence in the party because of its socially inclusive and pro-poor developmental philosophy of governance.

A political party in a democracy does not survive on the basis of its old achievements or moments of electoral glory. It has to perform for its survival and future electoral victories and the Congress party is not an exception to this general rule. The commitment of the Congress party led by Sonia Gandhi to India's future was clearly and unambiguously reflected in the annual budget of 2009-10 presented by finance minister Pranab Mukerjee. A few salient features of the annual budget indicate the direction towards which the country may be moving under the new UPA-II government.

It is for the first time in the history of post-independence India that an annual expenditure of more than ₹ 10 trillion has been proposed in the budget. Second, rural India, i.e., Bharat, is the focus of investments and the special focus is on the farmers and the poor. While farmers have been given an 'interest subsidy', the NREGS, the flagship programme of the Congress party, has received an amount of ₹ 39, 000 crore, an increase of 144 per cent from the budget of ₹ 16, 000 crore of 2008-09. Third, the focus is on Bharat Nirman, the rural housing fund, road connectivity, *et al.* The budget which is a political policy statement of the government is clearly focused on expanding the rural domestic market by creating purchasing power among the rural people.

India had begun its journey of planned economic development on the basis of an assumption that the benefits of economic growth will have a 'trickle-down-effect' and pull the people out of poverty. The new vision of the Congress party seems to be that it is only the 'bottom-up, socially inclusive approach' which will bring the 300 million or so people out of their existence below the poverty line.

The UPA government in its first term had launched the bold programme of NREGS. In its second avatar, the UPA government is taking the next step in the direction of welfare of the real poor in the form of the National Food Security Act. The government, on the basis of a parliamentary legislation, has decided to guarantee the supply of 25 kg of rice and wheat at ₹ 3 per kg to the 'rural and urban poor'. Jean Dreze, the eminent liberal economist, has stated that "the proposed right to food Act can be a solid complement to the NREGS".

While the right to employment to the rural poor is a prerequisite to create a sense of 'self-esteem and a feeling of dignity', the right to food is a must for survival.

Is it fair to maintain that the overall philosophical perspective of the Congress and the concrete budgetary allocations made by the finance minister provide enough evidence to characterise the Congress as a left-of-centre party? The left-of-centre approach towards governance is not foreign to the Congress party's thinking. It should not be forgotten that Jawaharlal Nehru's real legacy is the left-of-centre Congress party. Indira Gandhi also wore the mask of leftism as a tactic to confront and confound her opponents within her party.

Strong voices have been raised against the rural poor-oriented policies and budgetary allocations. Such pressure groups exist within and outside the Congress. No doubt, Sonia Gandhi has to manage contradictory pressures or lobbies which are operating against its socially inclusive growth policy. It is worth noting here that the communist parties can play a constructive role in support of the new social and economic policies especially those that are pro-poor and pro-rural development.

How can the Left not support NREGS? The Food Guarantee Act has been a demand of the democratic and leftist parties. The communists have already suggested that instead of the government's proposed scheme of 25 kg at ₹ 3 kg to the poor, their own preference is for the Antyodaya scheme which gives 35 kg of foodgrains at ₹ 2 per kg to those below the poverty Line. The Congress party and the communists can resolve this issue and make a grand success of the pro-poor food security Act.

This budget has taken the first bold step in focusing attention on rural economic growth. With pressure from socially progressive groups, the government can be pushed further to generate more 'purchasing power' in rural India. Though a centrist party like the Congress can always be pushed around by the Left or the Right depending on the role of various political forces which exist in the country, the Food Guarantee Act can become a pillar of the party's left-of-centre politics.

—1 August, 2009, The Economic Times

Politics of Social Sectarianism

Uttar Pradesh is trapped in a vicious circle of socio-economic and socio-cultural conflict and the politics we witness in this State is a mere reflection of this grim reality

The language used by Uttar Pradesh Congress chief Rita Bahuguna Joshi on July 15 and the political response by Chief Minister Mayawati to Ms Joshi's intemperate language clearly show that 'democracy by dialogue and dissent by reasoning' does not exist in the State. Politics of dialogue based on arguments in Uttar Pradesh is conspicuous by its complete absence from public life.

This is in uttar contrast with the belief that democracy is a system of governance where political participants are always actively engaged in dialogue and discussion on pubic issues and critics and political dissenters are able to freely argue their case with a view to arrive at a consensus on public issues.

Ms Mayawati herself is guilty of using language in public affairs which cannot bring any credit to any leader of a party or a Chief Minister of a State. More often she has targeted Mahatma Gandhi by using language which, to say the least, has been derogatory. Her latest contribution to anti-Gandhian vocabulary is that Gandhi was a 'natakbaz' and his concern for Dalits was a 'sham' and a 'drama'.

Incidentally, neither Kanshi Ram nor Ms Mayawati know about many other social reformers who fought against the evil of untouchability in society. It deserves to be clearly stated that it is historically wrong to maintain that only BR Ambedkar had fought for the cause and rights of the untouchables. Ambedkerites like Ms Mayawati need to be reminded of the historical context in which Gandhi fought for the rights of the Harijans (Dalits) when British colonial power was dividing the Indian society on the basis of caste.

British rulers patronised Ambedkar during the Round Table Conferences of the 1930s and Gandhi undertook fast unto death and compelled the rulers to give reservations to the Harijans under the Gandhi-Irwin Pact. This description is necessary to set the record straight because

Ms Mayawati has developed a habit of debunking Gandhi by choosing and using language which is not appropriate for any decent public discourse.

The larger analytical question is: Why has the level of public discourse and political culture in Uttar Pradesh sunk so low that dialogue is conducted in an idiom not worthy of the status held by leaders who are using these languages in politics and vitiating the atmosphere of public life?

Public life before and after independence in Uttar Pradesh saw constitutional debates in Legislative Assembly and struggles against colonial rule closer than most.

Men of letters like Munshi Prem Chand and institutions of culture like universities and colleges had contributed immensely to the overall cultural life of the State including politics. If one comes out of the nostalgia of the past, the deterioration has to be explained on the basis of overall political development of the State. An explanation which deserves to be completely rejected is that the present state of lack of political civility in the State can be attributed to the emergence of the politics of 'sub-altern classes' which has replaced 'elite politics' of the past. This explanation is unsustainable because the whole burden of deterioration in the standards of democratic debate has been shifted to the shoulders of the emerging Dalit and Backward Castes.

The focus is on the public conduct of leaders and not on the masses, and almost every political party and its leaders have contributed to the existing vitiated political culture in Uttar Pradesh. The growing trend of sectarian social divisions has given birth to an atmosphere of 'hate' and 'violence' against one another in the society. Ms Mayawati's often-repeated statements like 'Manuwadis' and her every attempt to create caste-versus-caste cleavages, an effort fully joined by Samajvadis like Mr Mulayam Singh has completely fragmented society and created a social milieu of one against the other on the basis of an enemy syndrome in society.

The deepening social sectarianisation in Uttar Pradesh has led to the overall backwardness of the State and the prevailing political culture represented by Ms Joshi, Ms Mayawati and others is a mere reflection of this. Not only this, the State has been trapped into a vicious circle of overall socio-economic and socio-cultural downfall which does not surprise one given the deterioration and vulgarisation of political idiom in the State. In these circumstances, even a civilised democratic dialogue cannot be initiated, leave all-round progress.

—6 August, 2009, The Pioneer

UPA's Drought of Governance

The media, the votaries of policies of economic liberalisation and privatisation of industrial and financial sectors of economy were hopeful that unlike the previous UPA Government, which was hamstrung by the presence of the Left, the Manmohan Singh Government in its second term would push further the policies of economic reform and liberalisation. But they were made to eat humble pie as all their hopes from the Government in power from the end of May to the middle of August have been completely belied.

The lacklustre performance of the Government in the first quarter of its second term is because of its incapability to provide meaningful leadership on national and international issues facing the country. Moreover, this time the Centre cannot blame the Opposition parties for following any obstructive approach.

Although Finance Minister Pranab Mukherjee said in the Lok Sabha that the first Budget session was very constructive because unlike local or parochial issues, members of Parliament had devoted their attention on issues of national and international concern, Railway Minister Mamata Banerjee staged a walk-out in protest against Government's proposed law on Land Acquisition at a formal meeting of the Cabinet.

The walk-out by a Cabinet Minister proves beyond any shadow of doubt that the Congress-led UPA coalition Government at the Centre consists of 'disparate groups' which have nothing in common and this coalition does not have any agreed common agenda of governance for the country. It clearly shows that the Government is bound to work on the basis of 'ad hocism' in governance.

Besides infighting, Prime Minister Manmohan Singh invited trouble for his Government at Sharm el-Sheikh in Egypt when he issued a joint statement with Pakistan Prime Minister Yousuf Raza Gilani on July 16 delinking the terror from composite dialogue. It will be wrong to maintain that only the Opposition parties reacted strongly against the statement. A divided Congress Party, and the country's public opinion also became antagonistic to the stand taken by Mr Singh while dealing with his Pakistani counterpart. A new Government which had already failed to make any mark on public affairs was faced with a shaky leader whose foreign policy came under scrutiny.

It was Mr Singh who suggested that a 100-day agenda of every Minister should be placed before public to convey the message that the new coalition Government means 'business' and people should judge it on the basis of its performance. The very intention behind the idea first 100-day agenda was laudable because well begun journey of a Government leaves a very positive impression on the people's consciousness. But this dream of the Prime Minister has disappeared in the thin air because coalition consists of 'disparate groups' without any thing in common among themselves and also because of his own poor start in his first foreign policy intervention with Pakistan.

Prime Minister's philosophical approach towards continuous and constant 'engagement' with Pakistan is laudable because the logic of proximity cannot be wished away. History and geography have a determining role in deciding the level of 'bilateralism'; however, foreign policy decisions have to be taken keeping the sentiments of people in mind.

The Prime Minister was caught on the wrong foot not on the issue of his approach based on continuous dialogue with Pakistan but on the operationalisation of policy at this moment because Indian public opinion is not favourable towards Pakistan.

The net result of acts of omission and commission of the Prime Minister, who has come to power for the second time, is that the first quarter of his Government has shown a condition of drought in policy making for the whole country.

—18 August, 2009, The Pioneer

Judicial Independence is Crucial

Every democratic country has evolved an extremely elaborate mechanism of ensuring 'accountability' of public decision-makers since every action of law makers and law enforcement agencies has an impact on the lives of millions of citizens. The constitutional system of checks and balances has proved inadequate to restrain the misuse and abuse of power by the powerful political executive and formidable bureaucracy. Therefore, many European countries have created an independent system of 'Ombudsman' for hearing complaints concerning misuse and abuse of power by public functionaries.

The need for enforcement of 'accountability' of public functionaries has been felt in India also. The Central Vigilance Commission was set up as early as mid-'60s. Later the institution of Lok Ayukta/Lok Pal too was created for the redressal of grievances of citizens, particularly with regard to the misuse of power by decision-makers. Another important step forward was taken in the first decade of the twenty-first century with the enactment of the Right to Information Act and the setting up of the Central Information Commission and State Information Commissions, to make government functioning transparent and accountable.

Of late, the demand has been raised that judges like Caesars' wife should be above suspicion and they should declare their 'assets' before taking the oath of office. While members of the Bench are reluctant, even hesitant, to place the list of their 'assets' before either the Central Information Commission or the minister of law or any other pubic institution, a powerful section of the bar, members of Parliament, and some retired judges are asking for public declaration of assets by the judges to gain people's trust.

However, the Judiciary as an independent institution of democracy is much more important than any system of regular scrutiny of the judges' assets by the public. The meaning of accountability of public functionaries cannot be properly understood without keeping in focus the 'role and functions' of various institutions of governance. The power exercised by the political executive and the proliferating bureaucracy is not at all comparable with the role and functions of the judges.

The Executive is omnipotent and omnipresent and if not controlled properly, it can victimise innocent citizens. The Judiciary does not have the reach of the Executive and this fact makes a qualitative difference between these institutions of governance in democracy. Not only this. The power of Executive is not at all comparable with that of the Judiciary because politicians and bureaucrats have complete control over fiscal and physical resources of the country.

This controlling power to allocate resources provides ample space and scope to the Executive to misuse and abuse public power at the cost of ordinary citizens for whom these resources are meant to be spent. Further, the bureaucracy, both civil and police, has the power to indulge in illegality to such an extent that basic liberties of ordinary citizens get denied. The only saviour in such a situation is the court of law.

Incidentally, Indians still have more confidence in the institution of Judiciary than any other institution of governance. That is why, for instance, after every inter-community riot, a judicial inquiry is demanded by the victims. After the complete failure of the political executive and civil and police bureaucracy to maintain law and order in Gujarat in March/April 2002, victims turned to the judiciary and not to the Executive, for safety of life, property and liberty.

Former Chief Justice PN Bhagwati introduced the system of Public Interest Litigation much before the RTI Act came into force, wherein an aggrieved citizen could approach the judiciary for redressal of grievances against the high-handedness of the Executive. Judicial interventions have brought relief, for example, to victims of fake encounters by the police, which is well known for its lawless approach even as it is expected to uphold the rule of law.

It is no one's case that judicial reforms should not be on the public agenda but in the case of Judiciary, if its independence gets compromised by any law, it will be a sad day for Indian democracy. Indians cannot forget the dark days of the Indira Gandhi regime of Emergency of 1975-77 when the Judiciary had gone into a 'coma'.

The proposed efforts to make the members of the Bench 'accountable' should be linked with surgical reforms of the Indian Bar which should be able to stand up and act as a 'watchdog' of integrity of the whole judicial system. It is very important to be cautious while dealing with the problems facing the Judiciary because unlike the Executive, and to some extent the Bar, the credibility of the judges is still quite high and this is the reason why the citizens look towards them for some relief. Ask victims of riots in India and they would vote for Judiciary and not the 'partisan' Executive.

—*22 August, 2009, The Economic Times*

A National Security State

A fundamental justificatory principle underpinning the operation of the post-Independence Indian state is that constitutionally guaranteed fundamental rights and civil liberties of citizens can be set aside, partially or fully, in the interest of safeguarding the external and internal security and territorial integrity of the country. In pursuit of this goal, the Indian state has equipped itself with extraordinary coercive laws to deal with individuals or groups branded by it as terrorists, insurgents, Maoists/Naxalites or secessionists.

On the eve of independence, the Indian nationalist leadership had promised that draconian anti-liberty laws of the colonial state like the Defence of India Rules would be thrown off the statutes because they run counter to the values of a Republican democratic country. In a cruel and ironic twist of history the post-Independence state broke its promise and 'detention without trial' of 'so-called' suspect citizens became a near norm rather than an exception. The journey started with the Preventive Detention Act, the Maintenance of Internal Security Act, the Unlawful Activities Prevention Act, 1967, the Terrorist Activities (Prevention) Act, 1987 (TADA), the Armed Forces (special powers) Act, the Prevention of Terrorism Act (POTA), among others, with all these special laws used at various times to 'detain people without proper trial'.

Hence, it is wrong to maintain that just as 11 September 2001 was the defining moment of the United States, the Mumbai terrorist attack of 26 November 2008 legitimised our putting the Unlawful Activities (Prevention) Amendment Act, 2008 (UAPA) and the creation of the National Investigation Agency Act, 2008 (NIA) which deal with the establishment of 'Special Courts' on the statute book.

It is not only the central government which has concentrated extraordinary legal authority to deal with so-called terrorists or secessionists or Naxalites, many state governments too have equipped themselves on the pattern of the central government with laws and special powers to deal with 'extraordinary criminals'. The best illustration of such a legal provision is found in the Maharashtra Control of Organized Crime Act (MCOCA).

The story does not end here. The states of Manipur and Jammu and Kashmir are covered by the Armed Forces (special powers) Act (AFSPA) granting the security forces complete 'immunity' to search a house without a warrant, arrest a suspect without giving any reason, or even eliminate a 'so called' terrorist. By placing on the statute book laws like the National Security Act and Unlawful Activities Act, the state feels free to violate every normal procedure of justice based on the rule of law in a democracy and seems to have completely immunized itself from its obligations to defend fundamental rights. Each of these laws contain provisions which violate the basic principle of natural justice, that no accused is guilty unless so determined by the due legal process. Such is the basic legal philosophy of a highly militarized and over-policed national security state.

Concomitant with this enabling legal architecture, the Indian state has invested heavily in creating military and paramilitary capability to deal with external and internal security threats. India has well-equipped professional armed forces along with the Central Reserve Police, the Border Security Force, the Central Industrial Security Force, among others, to confront various internal and external security challenges. Moreover, every state government too maintains its own state armed police forces which, when needed, can be supplemented by the central forces. Nevertheless, every time the state confronts a new challenge, for instance, moments like 26 November 2009, it responds by creating still another highly specialized paramilitary force like the National Security Guards, the anti-naxal Cobra battalions or the Greyhounds of Andhra Pradesh. It is worth noting that the combined budgetary allocation for defence and internal security has over time increased to a whopping ₹ 2, 00, 000 crore.

In sum, our security conscious state has rarely hesitated in disregarding the democratic rights and liberties of citizens in the belief that interests of state override the fundamental rights of citizens. Hence, the analytical question: Why does the Indian state feel the need for such draconian laws for dealing with various internal and external challenges? Does it really need more armed forces for dealing with domestic protests by citizens who may have decided to challenge the legitimacy of the state by taking recourse to the politics of the gun? Why does the Indian state follow the policy of bullet versus bullet when confronting gun wielding groups in society?

Evidently, our democratic rulers find it difficult to understand that only highly socially dissatisfied and disaffected groups eschew the path of democratic change through the ballot and take recourse to the politics of bullet. Both the President of India and the Prime Minister in their inaugural policy statements before the newly constituted fifteenth Lok Sabha have stressed that the Indian state will have to 'eliminate' the menace of left-wing extremism which has spread to West Bengal, Orissa, Jharkhand, Chhattisgarh, Andhra Pradesh among other states. Even as we believe that recourse to armed resistance is misdirected adventurism, the deep social reasons forcing discontented groups to take to the gun for a solution of their social problems cannot be wished away. It is not accidental that the Naxal affected districts of India are not only underdeveloped and backward, they are also inhabited by completely neglected tribal populations. Or that the presence of men in khaki uniform protected by the Armed Forces (special powers) Act in Jammu and Kashmir and Manipur generates hostility in the people of that region. Witness the thousands of people who regularly come out on the streets of Srinagar or Imphal to express their resentment against the many acts of omission and commission by our armed forces.

Our ruling classes need to do a lot of soul searching about the reasons of social discontent prevailing among different strata of the marginalized strata which compels them to take to guns against the state. The structural logic of exploitation, oppression, inequality and disparity creates a breeding ground for social alienation. Unfortunately the state, instead of understanding and responding to the causes of anger and alienation of multiple and diverse social groups, has created a sophisticated war machine to respond to even the legitimate grievances of the deprived strata of society. Instead of finding remedies to deal with the causes of such 'democratic deficit', they prefer to take recourse to repressive powers to elicit obedience from alienated citizens. It appears that every class-divided, oppressive capitalist society prefers quasi-authoritarian military apparatuses to confront the resentments of the underclass. The ongoing war against global terrorism post 9/11 has only provided a new alibi to state to equip itself with draconian laws for dealing with its own 'suspect' citizens.

—August, 2009, Seminar 600

Missing the Mark

Human Resource Development Minister Kapil Sibal, in his enthusiasm to reform the school education system, has decided to de-legitimise the time-tested high school examination by asking around 10, 000 Central Board of Secondary Education (CBSE)-affiliated schools to make Class X board examinations 'optional'.

The report of the Council of Boards of School Education (COBSE)—which represents over half a million schools—stated: 'There is no general consensus among Boards on making Class X exam optional at present.' Sibal followed it up by holding a meeting of the Central Advisory Board of Education, which also put a seal of approval on making the exam 'optional' for CBSE-affiliated schools.

The flimsy and non-academic argument is that Class X exams are 'stressful' for students. What's forgotten is that Class X students are mature enough to understand the advantages of an externally conducted examination. Incidentally, Sibal seems ignorant about the vagaries of the subjective factors involved in the process of 'internal assessment'.

Incidentally, the demand for making the board examination 'optional' hasn't originated from half a million school teachers. It has neither come from any other stakeholder nor from 'above' as a government dictum.

Further, Indian schools represent—even reflect—our national diversity. There is a reality which exists beyond CBSE-affiliated schools. Many children from lower middle- and middle-income groups receive formal education up to the tenth standard in schools located in small towns or semi-urban centres. These schools lack basic infrastructure and teachers, too, are ill-trained.

Also, a large number of students in these areas are 'first generation learners' and, so, require individual attention and extensive care. Thus, the need for an external examination by state education boards is felt in such schools because it creates a sense of discipline among teachers and prepares students for Class X board examinations.

This move will lead to confusion in schools where some students will go for the 'optional' exam and others would choose board examination. Will teachers teach two groups of students in one class? Is it a sound pedagogic system? The high school examination certificate carries a great tradition and is rooted in sound philosophy of the educational system. By focusing attention only on the CBSE schools, our policy makers are ignoring this reality.

This experiment should be put in cold storage and the system of examination by external agencies should continue at the school level. If the Class X examination is 'stressful', all examination systems should be abolished or made optional, for 'stress' is not restricted to high schools alone.

—1 September, 2009, The Hindustan Times

The Worrisome Babu-Neta Nexus

Chief Justice KG Balakrishanan has set the cat among the pigeons by making a public statement on September 12, 2009 that 'if a public official amasses wealth at the cost of the public, then the state is justified in seizing such assets.'

This made law minister Veerappa Moily to ask for a constitutional amendment and 'revisit' Article 311 of the Constitution which shields civil servants because they cannot be prosecuted without the prior approval of the government. The persistent and prevalent evil of corruption among civil servants has infected the whole body-politic and it deserves to be tackled very effectively.

The moot question is: can permanent government officials indulge in corrupt practices without the protective umbrella of politicians? Politicians in a democracy are the protectors and promoters of either corruption-free good governance or they are themselves engaged in governance based on the system of patronage.

Indian reality is that politicians have exercised their authority with a view to maximise their private benefit in cahoots with permanent officials. As a result, a nexus has developed between politicians and bureaucrats.

Corruption has eroded the moral foundations of the Indian state and society. And politicians and public servants have completely weakened the foundations of democracy based on the principle of rule of law and equality of every citizen before the law.

The Indian bureaucracy, headed by the IAS, the real Brahmans of the power structure, has played a relatively autonomous role whether during the period of economic planning or during the present phase of economic deregulation and liberalisation. The bureaucracy, especially the IAS, can bend or break any public policy according to their whims and fancies, as long as they enjoy the patronage of politicians.

How does the bureaucracy fit into the new administrative requirements of the phase of Economic Reform? Can the followers of regulatory procedures of the era of economic planning adapt themselves to the new ways of work required by the demands of a deregulated regime of economic growth?

The prime minister is worried because the bureaucracy is not able to deliver the services to the public under schemes launched for the aam aadmi. While the delivery of services to the targeted public is a legitimate concern of the PM, it also deserves to be mentioned that the same bureaucracy which is not responsive to the needs of common man, is quick to perform the work of the powerful strata of society.

It should not be forgotten that the higher echelons of bureaucracy, both at the Centre and at the level of state governments, have developed close linkages with other centres of power, especially in the new sectors of economy like telecommunication, petro-industry, and every upcoming infrastructural projects for development.

Big players are involved in the new sectors of the economy and these investors have shown immense capacity to 'co-opt and integrate' the public decision makers and a quid pro quo basis has been established between private business and industrial power centres and politicians and bureaucrats.

Many senior bureaucrats have migrated from public service to serve private Indian and foreign investors in the energy sector, telecommunications, and so on. Indian bureaucrats try to establish linkages with powerful private business elite while in public service by 'obliging' them at the cost of public interest and in return, the obliged big industrialists employ the kith and kin of the serving bureaucrats on lucrative terms and conditions.

Further, many important bureaucrats who have worked in crucial and critical ministries walk out of the government for lucrative private jobs. It's a worrisome situation that, of late, public bureaucracy has been privatised and has become the handmaiden of big Indian and foreign economic players.

This privatisation of public bureaucracy is at the cost of public interest because public policies are bent and broken to the benefit of favourites in industry. This development, dating back to the 1990s, deserves to be noticed because public policies and government decision-making cannot be left to bureaucrats who have become instruments in the hands of private business whose interests directly clash with public interests.

It is not only corruption, or casteisation or communalisation of bureaucracy but India has to be saved from its public servants who are at the beck and call of politicians and private powerful players whose interests are at variance with that of the government of the country.

The upshot of above narrative is that Indian bureaucracy has become an autonomous centre of power because of corrupt and obliging politicians who are fully linked with big business. This linkage of politician, bureaucrats and big business has corrupted the whole body politics of India. The cohabitation among these three powerful centres of power has adversely affected good governance in India.

—*3 October, 2009, The Economic Times*

Politics of Tokenism

The image of the Congress suffered a major setback when its much-touted programme of party leaders from Uttar Pradesh visiting Dalit homes on October 2 proved to be a sham affair. Interestingly, these leaders were asked by party general secretary Rahul Gandhi to spend a night at Dalit homes. But to the utter surprise to the heir apparent, State Congress leaders indulged in farcical activities while they were expected to live like Dalits.

The moot question is: Why is the Congress making efforts to reach Dalit constituencies in Uttar Pradesh? Why is Mr Gandhi making every effort to revive the Congress in the country's largest State?

Historically, the Congress has dominated the political scene in Uttar Pradesh both before independence and also during the post-independence years till 1980. But after that the party not only lost its supremacy in Uttar Pradesh, the impact of the erosion of its political strength was also felt at the Centre where the Congress lost power because out of the 84 Lok Sabha constituencies in undivided Uttar Pradesh, it could win in only a few of them in general elections after 1989-90.

The decline of the Congress in Uttar Pradesh led to its defeat not only in successive State Assembly elections but also at the Centre and it is only in the 2009 Lok Sabha election that the party can claim to have won a reasonable member of seats in the State. The Congress would like to consolidate its electoral support base in Uttar Pradesh and this is precisely why it is trying to win over its traditional supporters among Dalits and Muslims.

The Congress dominated Indian politics for about 40 years on the basis of support from higher castes, Dalits and Muslims in Uttar Pradesh, and it lost its appeal because Muslims walked away from it to Mr Mulayam Singh Yadav of the Samajwadi Party. Since 1995, Dalits have shifted their support to Ms Mayawati's BSP. If the Congress has to regain its hold over Uttar Pradesh, it has to contest against Ms Mayawati and Mr Singh and win back its traditional support base of Dalits and Muslims.

Unfortunately, while trying to do so, the Congress does not seem to have learnt from its past mistakes and is repeating its old story of 'tokenist' approach to win back the support of Dalits and Muslims. Is the Congress not responsible for the economic backwardness of the State? Dalits identified themselves with Ms Mayawati and abandoned the Congress in favour of their 'own' leader. The Congress, when in power, had put on the statute book a stringent law on atrocities committed against Dalits but it was implemented in a very half-hearted manner. The situation of Dalits under Ms Mayawati has not improved dramatically, however they have a subjective feeling of identification with their 'own' Dalit leader.

If Dalits were earlier disillusioned by the hollow promises made by the Congress Government in the State, they are still captivated by illusions about the idea of 'our' Government by Ms Mayawati and the Congress is finding an opening in the growing level of disillusionment with Ms Mayawati's shallow dramatic programmes. Hence, the Congress is serious in winning back the loyalty of Dalit voters and it is not without reason that Mr Gandhi is trying to revive the organisation in Uttar Pradesh.

An underdeveloped economy, Uttar Pradesh is a populous State where poverty is quite widespread among Dalits. Plight of Bundelkhand, a sub-region located between Uttar Pradesh and Madhya Pradesh, shows how due to complete neglect of successive State Governments during the last 60 years the poor have been compelled to sell their womenfolk for their livelihood and survival. Some regions of the State are extremely backward and in such a situation voters are shifting their support and loyalty to one party after another so that the party in power can provide them with better amenities.

In this multi-polar politics Congress has identified Dalits and Muslims as its potential supporters. Uttar Pradesh voters have tried the Congress, the BJP, the SP and now the BSP and through a method of trial and error, they have settled down on the fractured politics of caste versus caste. In these circumstances, is there any hope for non-sectarian politics in the State?

Uttar Pradesh has seen more gimmickry in politics than any other State and if on the one hand Mr Gandhi-led Congressmen are expected to win over Dalits by identifying with their daily living situation, on the other, Ms Mayawati for the last two years has played her cards by erecting statues and monuments. The Congress and the BSP are competing against each other on the basis of empty shell of political drama and neither has presented an alternative model of economic development to the Uttar Pradesh electorate.

The Congress is trying to woo the Dalit voters in the State by using old tricks but has forgotten that much has changed since when it used to be power and now the voter is not ready to re-elect a party which is seen as a 'cheater'. The party should remember that political appeal during one election cannot bring political dividends in the next election if the party in-power or in-opposition has not implemented in a concrete manner the promises made during the elections.

—20 October, 2009, The Pioneer

Uniformly Bad across States

Though north Indian States are routinely criticised for being underdeveloped, States in south India are no better. The latter would do well to realise this fact

The epithet of BIMARU States is reserved for Rajasthan, Uttar Pradesh, Bihar, Madhya Pradesh, Jharkhand, Chhattisgarh and Uttarakhand because each of these States sorely lag behind others in most of the development indices. These north Indian States are guilty of mis-governance and non-governance which have led to their underdevelopment and backwardness. North Indians in general have had a lion's share in power at the Centre and except PV Narasimha Rao and a short stint by Mr HD Deve Gowda, all Prime Ministers in post-independence India have been from north India. And these Prime Ministers have been generous in dealing with the fiscal requirements of north India. Hence, if some north Indian States have earned the title of BIMARU States while south Indian States have been highlighting their economic success stories, it is because the latter have escaped critical scrutiny, since the media has always focussed on the former.

Politics in south Indian States is as good or bad as that in north Indian States. A few facts may be mentioned to substantiate this argument. First, south Indian States are no exceptions to dynastic politics which is a nationwide problem. Mr M Karunanidhi, the Chief Minister of Tamil Nadu and a senior patron of Dravidian politics, is not shy of promoting his extended family members in politics of his State. Andhra Pradesh and Karnataka, whether they are under Congress-led or BJP-led State Governments, still suffer from the 'Reddy effect'. The unfortunate death of Andhra Pradesh Chief Minister YS Rajsekhara Reddy led to a ruckus within the Congress because the late Reddy's son, a green horse in politics, mobilised party supporters to acquire the top political office in the State. It created a major problem for the central Congress leadership until it chose Mr K Rosaiah to head the State Government.

The impact of the powerful Reddy's of Andhra Pradesh was felt recently in neighbouring Karnataka where the bone of contention was the way in which the Yeddyurappa-led State Government was dealing with Janardhana Reddy and his brother's companies like Obula Puram Mining Company. Incidentally, the Reddy brothers have vast business interests not only in Karnataka but also in Andhra Pradesh. They exercise great clout over both State Governments.

The Karnataka Chief Minister had imposed a cess of ₹ 1, 000 on every truck load of iron ore. This had hit the business interests of the Reddy brothers adversely. In retaliation they compelled the Chief Minister to withdraw this cess and appoint only those bureaucrats in their areas of operation whom the brothers wanted.

Political power for personal profits has become an all-India phenomenon. The south Indian State Governments are openly practicing and following this national norm. Hence, South India is no different from other States like Jharkhand where the Koda scandal has surfaced. Every State Government in the country has politicised the bureaucracy and political favourites are routinely picked from the group of obliging bureaucrats. Karnataka Chief Minister BS Yeddyurappa was made to eat humble pie by the Reddy brothers because he had transferred obliging civil servants from the latter's area of operation.

Therefore, it is uncharitable to suggest that the BIMARU States of north India are guilty of mis-governance and non-governance, whereas, south Indian States are shining examples.

If Uttarakhand, Chhattisgarh and Jharkhand had to be created because these regions felt neglected in the large underdeveloped States of Uttar Pradesh, Madhya Pradesh and Bihar respectively, the Telangana region of so-called developed Andhra Pradesh is also fighting for separate Statehood.

If Andhra Pradesh is truly so developed, why can't it take care of all its sub-regions? Further, every large federal country has relatively more developed and less developed regions. India is no exception to this rule. A responsive, democratic Union Government is expected to evolve special policies and programmes for backward States and regions. India will develop only if every State has reached a reasonable level of development. The States of South India, instead of basking in their achievements, should realise that in many essential ways they are no different from the BIMARU States. The States of south India are not free from the disease of dynastic politics or the corrupting role of money in politics. The politics of unity in diversity can succeed only if all regions have mutual respect, and disparaging remarks are not used against Hindi-wallah States.

—17 November, 2009, The Pioneer

Beyond Caste-Based Identity Politics

The founding fathers of secular democratic Republic had expected that the right to equality given to every citizen along with the institutional system of universal adult franchise will lay down the foundations of a new social and political order where fragmented, parochial and narrow caste-and sub-caste based identities will become completely redundant. The basic philosophical premise of the Indian constitution makers was that universal fundamental rights given to every citizen irrespective of their caste or creed will eventually lead to the emergence of casteless society whose foundational principle will be equal opportunity for everyone as a citizen and even reservations for the SCs and STs was just a 'transitory' concession based on a commitment that caste-based rights will never become an integral part of public policy and governmental decisions. Nehru's government concretised the philosophical ideas of universality of citizenship by launching programmes and plans of economic and social development for the whole society. It was not only governmental policies of Nehru's era which were meant for the uplift and welfare of the people of India, Congress party also mobilized the voters by creating a broad social platform of all castes, communities and religions from Kashmir to Kohima. It was not only that Nehru dedicated developmental projects like steel plants or Big Irrigation Dams to the 'nation' and not to any single section of society, the Congress party also played its political role by mobilizing every strata of society for electoral support and in the process, the Congress social base became 'socially all-inclusive'.

The moral of the story is that Nehru's phase of politics has clearly shown that the path of economic development for the whole society can pay great political dividends not only in terms of electoral victories but also for laying down the foundations of a modern casteless society especially for the poor laboring under classes. The caste-based identity politics can become completely irrelevant if an all-India national party practices the politics of programmes and policies for the development of the whole society. Indira Gandhi's slogan of 'Garibi Hatao' had brought political and electoral support from every strata of society especially women because everyone identified himself or herself with Indira's programme of social progress. This is only one part of the story. Much water has flown down the Ganges when national mobilization took place around national plans and programmes of economic development and national parties could mobilize the voters without appealing to their narrow, parochial and sectarian identities like caste or sub-caste or religion or language. A few facts may be mentioned to substantiate the argument that the political space vacated by programme and policy centred practitioners of national politics has been occupied by the champions of sectarian caste-based parties and politics. First, North Indian politics witnessed a phase of complete break from the past when V.P. Singh, to safeguard his Prime Ministership in 1989-90, announced the acceptance of Mandal Commission Report on Reservations for the Backward castes. The Lok Sabha and State Assembly elections were not only contested on caste versus caste mobilizational strategies, caste, politics and parties also became 'indistinguishable' and numerically dominate castes captured the levers of power and Chief Ministers and government were just an extension of Yadavas or Kurmis or Jatava Dalit *et al.*

Second, the gradual process of the weakening of Congress party also made it dependent on assured caste-based social constituencies for winning State Assembly elections. The Maratha caste in Maharashtra, the Lingayyats and Vokkaligas in Karnataka and Kammas and Reddys in Andhra Pradesh became politically decisive factor numerically and socially powerful castes could win an election. Elections became a contest between castes and not between parties and programmes. The Reddys of the Congress or a section of Reddy and Kammas of Telugu Desam of Chandra Babu Naidu have reduced political contest in Andhra Pradesh between the same caste groups. Tamil Nadu's post-independence politics is a child of anti-Brahmin movement and it is the backward or Most backward or Dalit castes which are mobilized by the Congress, the DMK, the AIADMK or other pure sub-caste based parties like the PMK of the Vanniyars. The above narrative clearly shows that caste or sub-caste based sectarian politics has become an all-India phenomenon and all-India parties are making their own caste-based calculations for electoral purposes. Is there a way out of the growth of caste-based sectarianism in politics? The battle is not fully lost. Sonia's Congress party by reviving the social and ideological pro-poor developmental programme of Nehru era Congress can re-create a non-caste and non-sectarian social-national platform. During his visit to Uttar Pradesh, Rahul Gandhi hinted at such a possibility on December 7, 2009 when he stated that 'The funds spent on installing statues in this state are higher than those earmarked for universities'. He further stated 'we want to change politics here... The politics of caste or temples is over. Now issues like jobs, education and health alone with matter.' This is Nehru's language where ideological politics had superseded sectarian social categories like caste or community based identity politics. The Voting Studies have shown that even when Congress party was out of power for about last two decades the majority of poor had voted for the party.

This is social capital on the basis of which ideological politics can be built by the Congress with a goal to bring 'Aam Admi' in the Centre stage without attaching any label of caste of community around him. It is not only Congress, ideologically cadre based pro-poor communist parties can also make caste-based politics completely irrelevant and redundant. It also deserves to be stated that parties like the DMK or the AIADMK or the Telugu Desam or the Congress which are mobilizing castes for electoral victories have great potential of liberating themselves from their social constituencies because they are political parties in the real sense of the term and they are not just an 'extension' of their caste based support structure. Unlike North Indian casteist parties which are just an extension of caste identity, political parties in the South can win an election on the basis of an agenda of purposive politics not confined to any particular caste. The upshot of above narrative is that secular, forward looking pro-poor programmatic parties can restore the preeminent position of politics of nation-building and completely replace the present system of caste-based or Hindu-religion divisive and based destructive politics of the country.

— *19 December, 2009, The Economic Times*

How not to Solve a Problem

The Congress has completely messed up the situation in Andhra Pradesh on the issue of a separate Telangana State. It is a democratic right of political parties — in Government or in Opposition — to negotiate and find solutions to any complex problem. Hence, it has come as a surprise that the Congress-led Government at the Centre has not been able to tackle the agitation over Telangana.

Not only this, following Home Minister P Chidambaram's announcement that steps to form the State of Telangana will be initiated, Telangana Rashtra Samithi chief K Chandrasekhar Rao called off his fast unto death in December. All hell broke loose after Mr Chidambaram's announcement as allies of the UPA Government and, other national and regional parties reacted very strongly either in favour or against Telangana. Ms Mamata Banerjee's Trinamool Congress and Sharad Pawar's NCP, key allies of the UPA Government, strongly opposed the idea of bifurcation of Andhra Pradesh. The CPI(M) too echoed the same view.

While the CPI(M) and the Trinamool Congress are worried about the demand for a separate Gorkhaland, the NCP and the Shiva Sena are concerned about the separation of Vidarbha from Maharashtra.

Moreover, the NCP also flayed the Union Government for not consulting coalition partners before making such an important policy announcement. This implicitly suggests that the Congress had not followed coalition dharma and in the process it has created confusion worse confounded.

It was expected of the Centre to take an all-India perspective while dealing with the demand of a particular region. It decided to call a meeting of all political parties on January 5 to evolve a national consensus on the issue but this belated exercise failed because neither national parties nor regional parties were ready to support the Centre's ill-considered decision on Telangana.

The Centre realised its folly when the TRS and the votaries of separate Telangana took out a victory procession which was followed by anti-Telangana processions.

Moreover, the city of Hyderabad, once an investment destination, has come to a standstill as violent demonstrations — both in favour and against of Telangana — have become a daily routine with projects, orders and investments being cancelled across sectors. Even the venue of the Confederation of Indian Industry Partnership Summit 2010, scheduled later this month, has been shifted from Hyderabad to Chennai. It is to be realised that capital investment is very mobile and if Hyderabad is not an attractive place for investors, they will move to other States the way West Bengal has lost the Tata Nano project to Gujarat.

However, the Andhra Pradesh Government is now trying for an investment summit instead.

It's the time that the Centre and the State Government take measures to check the deteriorating law and order situation in Andhra Pradesh. Besides, the UPA Government must keep in mind that governance in coalition politics is quite different from the Congress's rule 40 years ago.

It was expected that the Manmohan Singh Government would have learnt lessons from its past blunders when it unnecessarily mentioned the issue of Balochistan in the India-Pakistan joint statement at a bilateral meeting in Sharm el-Sheikh on the sidelines of the Non-Aligned Movement summit last year.

Furthermore, the Centre should have been sensitive to the issue of regional and sub-regional sentiments which will be aroused by any decision on Telangana without national consensus.

It's time the Congress-led UPA Government asks itself: Is it governance when a solution to a problem complicates the situation instead of resolving the issues?

—12 January, 2010, The Pioneer

Social Inclusion: A Wasted Year

A self-assured Congress party launched its second journey in 2009, securing 207 seats, compared to 147 in 2004 in the Lok Sabha, with reduced dependence on allies. Moreover, if from a position of weakness, the Congress-led UPA government from 2004 to 2009 could launch a mega pro-poor programme, the National Rural Employment Guarantee Scheme, the relatively-stronger Congress in 2009 could give a big push to social inclusion.

The Congress claimed, in its Lok Sabha elections manifesto of 2009, that only it had an agenda of inclusive growth for the whole of India, specifically targeting the socially-excluded groups bypassed by the trickle-down theory.

Hence, Congress came out with a revolutionary programme of reservation of 33 per cent seats for women in the Lok Sabha and the state assemblies. Sonia Gandhi employed her political energy and the Womens Reservation Bill was approved in the Rajya Sabha in 2010. The Congress party was confident that with the support of the BJP and the Communists, it will be able to get a seal of approval in the Lok Sabha. However, the Bill could not be introduced.

The real pro-poor programme of food security for below-poverty-line rural and urban population has not reached Parliament and it is bogged down in usual bureaucratic discussions on the actual number of people who are below the poverty line.

The most important programme of social inclusion in a country inhabited by a large majority of rural and urban poor is to guarantee provision of food to the vulnerable and deprived population. It deserves to be mentioned that democratic governments, even in developed countries, have recognised that the right to food, right to work and right to health are to be guaranteed and ensured by public authorities.

Why has the Congress-led UPA government spent the whole year of 2009 to 2010 to legislate on National Food Security Law It does not bring credit to anyone, least to the Prime Ministers Office, if Sonia Gandhi has to castigate the government for its failure to bring before Parliament a Bill for a guaranteed right to food promised by the Congress manifesto of 2009.

Finally, after wasting the whole year of 2009 to 2010, the government has opted for Tendulkar committees figure of 41 per cent rural population as below poverty line. It is ironic that in a country where huge percentage of food grain is wasted and not distributed among the starving and semi-starving population because the government has inadequate arrangements for its storage year after year. It has been alleged that the Manmohan Singh government has spent more political energy in dealing with the controversial Civil Liability for Nuclear Damage Bill, 2010, than on seeing through the passage of Food Security Bill in Parliament.

It is only on May 7, 2010, that the government has pushed through the Lok Sabha its Bill on Nuclear Damage. The UPA government has completely wasted its first year in office by not even finalising the most important social agenda of food security.

The story of the stalled project of social inclusion does not begin or end here. The 21st-century India is witnessing large-scale displacement of rural population from land that is required for mega industrial projects like the setting up of steel plants in Orissa and other states where iron ore is available. The government, especially state governments, are acquiring land for big business for special economic zones and millions of rural poor are getting displaced from their land with a promise of resettlement of those who are evicted.

Industrialisation and extraction of rich mineral wealth from the countrys dense forest belt, which is inhabited by large forest-dependent tribal population, makes victims of the inhabitants. The UPA government and state governments have evicted people from land in spite of Forest Dwellers Act and other legal provisions that guarantee legal rights to socially-excluded groups for a legitimate share in the fruits of economic growth of the first decade of the 21st century.

Social inclusion project is an ideological and political commitment. The Congress has not moved an inch forward because as a party, it is not really committed to the implementation of programmes targeted for the excluded tribals and others living below the poverty line. The Congress is living in a fools paradise if it thinks that by exercising governmental powers, it can achieve its social goals because merely putting laws on the statute book, no party can achieve its comprehensive social agenda for inclusion of millions of excluded poor who have already missed the bus.

Politics is the main, even primary, force that mobilises deprived social groups to demand from the government implementation of its promises made through laws approved by Parliament. The Congress as a party has not mobilised those who have been evicted from land and have not been resettled because in the absence of political backing, a powerful nexus of bureaucrats, contractors and big business acts as a road block to include the excluded law alone cannot guarantee that citizens can realise their rights.

The Congress party has not shown capacity to provide political muscle power behind its governments programme of social inclusion and is satisfied with putting laws on the statute book, especially those concerning the excluded. Law is only an instrument of the government, its impact cannot be felt by the poor if flesh and blood is not provided by political and ideological commitment of the political class.

—22 May, 2010, The Economic Times

Enter Coalition Compromise, Exit Ideology

Many laudatory commentaries have been made on the emergence of the phase of coalition Governments and the end of the dominance of the Congress party. It was felt that a coalition Government, unlike the centralised Congress system of governance, would be accommodative of the democratic aspirations of multiple social groups and diverse regions of the country.

An apprehension was also expressed that the coalition Governments would be unstable because unlike the Congress Governments of 40 years of independent India, the coalitions may break up because of inner contradictions among the partners. A few facts may be mentioned to demystify the reality and the inner story of the working of coalition Governments at the Centre. A new idiom was added in the dictionary of democratic politics when a party with a miniscule minority formed the Central Government with the 'outside support' of parties to manufacture a majority in the Lok Sabha.

It is a caricature of the parliamentary system of democracy where political groups form a Government with the support of parties which enjoy immense power over the Council of Ministers without owning any responsibility for the acts of omission and commission of the Government. The 'outside supporters' also get rewards by being close to the power-that-be.

Further, the coalition phase of the Government at the Centre has given birth to the phenomena of complete 'non-ideologisation' of politics. Groups with opposing ideologies have entered into a marriage of inconvenience and joined Governments led by the BJP or the Congress. George Fernandes, Ram Vilas Paswan, Nitish Kumar, Sharad Yadav *et al* have supported Right-wing forces while pretending to be socialist and secularist. Ms Mamata Banerjee, Mr M Karunanidhi and Ms Mayawati have not hesitated to be part of the BJP government, and on the drop of the hat, have joined the bandwagon of the Congress-led UPA Government without any embarrassment.

Thus the stark political reality of all coalition governments at the Centre has been that 'autonomous' political groups, without any commonality, joined together to form a coalition Government with the sole purpose of siphoning of public resources for their own specific constituencies and also with a view to win a few seats in the Lok Sabha for getting a ministerial berth. The coalition era of politics has witnessed the arrival of non-ideological, unprincipled, heterogeneous groups bound together with the sole goal of entering the corridors of power as Ministers and act as independent shareholders in a coalition Government. The Council of Ministers does not have any primary or controlling centre of authority because the Prime Minister is not even *primus inter pares* vis-à-vis Ministers as the representation in the Cabinet is quota-based and Ministers representing a political group are absolutely under the thumb of their leader.

If this hypothesis is nearly approximation to reality, the coalition Government at the Centre, whether of the BJP-led NDA or the Congress-led UPA consists of nearly 'autonomous' groups whose ministers because of their loyalty and commitment to their leader do not hesitate to exercise their ministerial power for the promotion of their own interests. Further, every political group represented in the coalition Government has to win elections on its own without any linkage with other members of the coalition. Hence, every political group has to exercise his power for the collection of funds for elections and in the process, Ministers bend public policies which can bring financial benefits for their own separate group. Mr A. Raja, the Telecom Minister in the UPA Government, does not hesitate to collect funds for the DMK inspite of allegation that private funds were collected in the allocation of 2-G spectrum.

Ms Jaya Jaitley of the George Fernandes' Janata Party as a partner of BJP-led NDA coalition Government was caught collecting funds in the official residence of the then Defence Minister. Mr Madhu Koda and Mr Shibu Soren are a 'star performers' supported by BJP or Congress as Chief Ministers of coalition. Further, every political party is tightly controlled by a 'supremo.' The supremo is the sole controller of party funds. Coalition Governments consist of 'Little Napoleons' who control their little principalities by controlling "funds" on the basis of their power to distribute patronage. Every "partner" in a coalition colludes and cooperates with everyone else and even CBI investigations into corruption cases of political supporters are dispensed with.

—15 June, 2010, The Pioneer

UPA-II: Searching for Direction

The Congress felt liberated after the Lok Sabha election results of 2009, and on the basis of its own sizeable strength of 207 MPs, it developed a feeling that it will be in the driver's seat in the new United Progressive Alliance (UPA) coalition government of 2009.

But its dream lay shattered within the very first week of Cabinet formation when its new major coalition partners not only dictated the terms of their representation , but also asserted their right to allot portfolios of choice for their nominees.

Even as A Raja of the DMK is constantly under a cloud for his handling of 2G spectrum auction of telecom operations, the prime minister cannot ask for any explanation from his own minister. To top it all, DMK chief M Karunanidhi arrives in Delhi to make a statement that Raja, as telecom minister, is under attack because he is a Dalit.

The story does not end here.

If the coalition partners are pursuing their own party agendas as Cabinet ministers and are acting autonomously of the authority of the PM, ministers of the Congress party do not feel constrained either by their own party discipline or authority of their own PM and freely express in public their differences on policy matters that have been agreed upon by the government.

Jairam Ramesh goes to China to discuss issues concerning the environment and the Copenhagen agreement, but makes a statement against the policies of his own government involving the management of ministries of home and defence by publicly alleging that 'our security establishment's overtly defensive and alarmist approach towards China' is acting as a roadblock to the development of fruitful economic bilateral relations.

The utter lack of coordination within the UPA government along with a feeling that the PM's writ does not run with his ministerial colleagues is reflected in the government's response to the Maoist challenge. The Congress party is speaking in differing idioms on the issue of the challenge posed by Maoists.

When in Chhattisgarh, a suggestion was made by a responsible minister of the government that the 'army should be deployed and the help of the air force should be taken to confront the Maoists'. The army chief and AK Antony, the defence minister belonging to the Congress party, nipped this irresponsible idea in the bud. This confusion on the anti-Maoist strategy continues to persist within the government as revealed during the June 10 meeting of the Cabinet ministers.

Mr Chidambaram has repeatedly stated that 'economic development' is possible only when the government is able to establish its domination over the Maoists. The contrary view within the Congress leadership is that without tackling the root causes, which have given birth to Maoism, only a law-and-order approach cannot bear fruit.

Sonia Gandhi herself has come out in public against the 'law-and-order approach first and development afterwards' line while responding to the ongoing debate. In the latest issue of Congress party journal Sandesh, she described Naxalism an 'enormous challenge' and went on to state that 'we have to address the root causes of Naxalism.

The rise of Naxalism is a reflection of the need for our development initiatives to reach the grassroots, especially in our most backward tribal districts.' Sonia, Digvijay Singh, Mani Shankar Aiyar *et al.* are openly saying that Chidambaram's approach will not succeed in silencing the guns of the Maoists.

The Congress leaders are themselves suggesting that the Centre should overcome its complacency and launch a big drive for the protection of 'the rights of forest dwellers' and the Centre should directly deal with the problem because it has powers under the Constitution's Fifth Schedule areas and also actively involve the Panchayats under the 1996 law of the Panchayats (Extension to Scheduled Areas) Act (PESA).

The above description clearly shows that on an important policy issue like the Maoist challenge, the Congress party as leader of the UPA government is totally confused. The party has shown vacillation and ambivalence in the implementation of its own agenda of social inclusion, and it brings no credit to the Congress leadership the way it allowed its own secular agenda of 33 per cent reservation for women in the Lok Sabha and the state assemblies to be completely hijacked and derailed by casteist leaders like Lalu Prasad Yadav, Mulayam Singh, Sharad Yadav and Mayawati.

The Congress-led UPA parties do not have a common manifesto or agenda for governance. It brings no credit to the prime minister when Sonia Gandhi writes an open letter and asks for an agreed percentage of people below the poverty line for the implementation of the proposed National Food Security Act.

And after this letter, the government has to take a relook at the BPL figures. This brings us to the crux of the issue: what is the explanation for this complete directionlessness? The lacklustre press conference of the PM and presentation of UPA's record of one year on May 31 clearly showed that vacillation is the central characteristic of this government.

The Congress party agenda of reservation for women or Nation Food Security or Right to Free and Compulsory Education for all children between the age of 6 and 14 years remains a pipe dream and confusion on major policies is reflected when one hears different voices of ministers in their public statements. That a dualism of authority within the Congress actually operates is clearly substantiated by the presence of the Sonia Gandhi-led National Advisory Council with the strength of a secretariat of 35 members and 14 'good persons' who will decide about the welfare of the nation. It is clear that the supreme leader of the Congress will keep a watchful eye on the functioning of the government.

The prime minister and Cabinet ministers in a modern complex parliamentary democracy have enough agencies that are directly working under them for proving policy inputs to the government. Hence, Sonia Gandhi-led National Advisory Council constituted on June 1 is either irrelevant for the purposes of government, or it is much more than the mystified description of an advisory council. The Manmohan Singh government while making public policies would have to look behind its shoulders before a crucial public policy is announced. How can a government that acts under such fetters lead the country?

— 19 June, 2010, The Economic Times

Case Census and its Implications

Saturday Special this week has been conceived against the caste conundrum currently sweeping northern India. It is a storm with more than one eye and no follower of the rhetoric can avoid asking the obvious question: where does this lead India? At this time, a book by Rajesh Shukla, Caste in a Different Mould: Understanding the Discrimination (Business Standard publication, 2010, ₹ 895) has appeared to place the citizen-consumer's position in perspective. This is the first attempt by a scholar to use a cross-country sample to quantify the impact of education, urbanisation and occupation on the income levels of different caste groups. Shukla, as Chief Statistician of the National Council of Applied Economic Research (NCAER) and now Director of NCAER-Centre for Macro Consumer Research, has powered his book with data from India's premier economics think tank. One of the many useful characteristics of this book is variegated data on how caste categories are economically faring in contemporary India, particularly under reservation policies.

Has caste-based reservations substantively raised the level of lives led by the so-called 'backwards'? In a summer dominated by news about "honour killings", this question receives no attention at all. We present Mirza Asmer Beg, a Professor with Aligarh Muslim University, who described the core reasons supporting the birth and flourishing of identity politics, namely the arguable fruits of reservation. It would be wrong, he writes to focus on only the deprivation faced by the so-called lower castes because it camouflages other kinds of discriminations like economic poverty, which may or may not be truly consistent with caste.

As if casteism in politics and economics was not enough, the leaders of modern India have now stretched the debate to bizarre heights by seeking to revive the caste-based Census enumeration policy which was given up 80 years back by India's British masters. By proposing to institutionalising enumeration by caste, the leaders behind the move would also be committing the inappropriate act of giving acknowledgment to a term—caste—which the Constitution of India has consciously refused to recognise. The Constitution has used the word 'caste' only twice—in Articles 15 and 16—to forbid the State from practicing discrimination on the basis of caste, creed, race, sex, etc. While the founding fathers did issue the term 'Scheduled Caste', but in a restricted context.

The post-Independence State has consciously followed public policies which have institutionalised and solidified anachronistic inherited systems of Jatis, up-Jatis (castes and sub-castes) because the real consequence of caste-based "preferential policies", popularly known as "Politics of reservations" is that the State has accorded a "legal" status to the hoary tradition of hereditary castehood.

If the Constitution of India provides every citizen a few fundamental rights without any consideration or difference based on religion, caste, creed and gender, the makers of public policy are guilty of ignoring some fundamental principles of equality. The process of casteisation of society by political parties appears unstoppable and the latest nail in the coffin of the idea of an egalitarian India is the proposal (or demand) to conduct Census 2011 along caste line.

It deserves to be clearly stated that our British colonisers had initiated the practice of having caste-based headcounts, which they themselves discontinued in 1931. They found that caste-based data cannot be authentically collected by enumerators during the Census exercises. It was logical for the British colonisers to identify Indians along caste lines they London perceived India as a fragmented nation. It also suited their divide-and-rule policy.

How the governments of free India could dumbly toe the coloniser's line is a matter of mystery. While formulating their public policies they kept in mind only "sectional interests" of castes and communities. If such a definition of India is accepted by every political party or group or leader, it is logical to pursue this approach. So the Census of 2011 should be conducted by enumerating the thousands of castes and sub-castes of fragmented India. The thousands of fragmented Jatis and up-Jatis should be documented by the Census officials.

It is not without reason that casteist political leaders like Lalu Prasad, Sharad Yadav and Mayawati, along with sectarian Congressmen like Veerappa Moily and BJP leaders like Gopinanth Munde are pushing for this retrogressive system. It deserves to be stated that the idea of a caste-based Census was not on the agenda of the Congress, the BJP and

Communists. It has been forced on the nation's psyche by the beneficiaries of caste-versus-caste politics, the same who have mobilised the Yadavs, Jats, Kurmis, Gujjars, etc. They are out to superimpose the coloniser's perception mixed with narrow, domestic sectarianism. The logical interpretation of identifying every individual on the basis of 'caste by birth' is that instead of an all-India nationalistic consciousness, what is promoted is caste-based customs, caste-based symbols and caste-based loyalties.

Why has a socially regressive and reactionary demand like caste-based enumeration been raised by the casteist political formations? The answer to that is obvious—seek out more issues for sustenance. They expect the Census process to come out with revelations of more caste groups being poor or backward or needy of reservations. They hope to win extended stays for themselves in the political arena by picking up these nuggets of information and converting them into noisy slogans. The story will not end there. Without waiting for the tabulation and scientific analysis of the Census data, these leaders would court voters using greater reservations as a plank.

The upshot is that notwithstanding caste-based censuses, a proper enumeration by caste may never be possible. This is because when the enumerator, usually a schoolteacher, goes out to fill the forms, there would be no option but record whatever the respondent householder states as the caste formation of the family. This cannot be verified because the enumerator is unlikely to be coached with information about local variants of caste nomenclature. Besides, it would take years of solid analysis to collate the information collected from various parts of India owing to the diversity of sub-castes and their changed profile from region to state. A caste may be considered 'backward' in one state, but not so in another. So, a national census would produce very confusing data sets, which is definitely not good for policy formulation.

But our casteist politicians are not interested in the science of caste-based enumeration. They are only interested in creating vote banks by promising caste-based benefits by the governments controlled by them. Casteism and fragmentation of society are not the concerns of Indian political leaders till they manage to win an election and govern on the basis of quid pro quo with caste groups.

Caste-based census results give politicians the opportunity to duck out from their duties to the larger nation. They begin to operate in a narrow channel and Indian laws would soon resemble the diktats of caste panchayats. Civil society everywhere in India has reacted with horror to the Indian State's veritable suicidal step of officially dividing up its citizens. What next? Caste-based electorates?

—26 June, 2010, The Pioneer

Do-gooders Step into Government's Shoes

Prime Minister Manmohan Singh, in consultation with UPA chairperson Sonia Gandhi, picked up 14 members for the National Advisory Council. It has been stated that these 14 'wise men' of Ms Gandhi will act as the UPA2 Government's 'Planning Commission for Social Agenda'.

Under the chairmanship of Ms Gandhi, these 14 experts will 'steer the welfare policies of the Government'. Many questions have arisen about the very idea of non-political individuals acting as friend, philosopher and guide to the political executive in a parliamentary democracy. It is the Council of Ministers headed by the Prime Minister which is accountable to the Parliament for all its policies, programmes and overall functioning of the Government.

Ms Gandhi was elected the Congress president on April 6, 1998. It was she who singlehandedly brought about a turnaround in the party's fortunes. Successive electoral victories in 2004 and 2009 and formation of two Congress-led coalition Governments at the Centre have made Ms Gandhi a centre of power. The party has accepted her as its supreme leader.

Like any other party, the Congress has every right to elect Ms Gandhi as president. The Congress-led UPA Governments of 2004 and 2009 could have elected her as Prime Minister. The only point of contention is that Ms Gandhi is not the Prime Minister but, as president of the Congress, exercises full authority over the Prime Minister and his Council of Ministers.

Does Ms Gandhi's status as overseer diminish the Prime Minister's authority? Does the NAC limit the political authority of the Prime Minister and his Council? It is a known fact that the Government brought a Bill for 33 per cent of reservation for women in Lok Sabha and State Assembly seats only on Ms Gandhi's initiative. Ms Gandhi was given full credit for the Bill and the Prime Minister and other members of the UPA Government were merely asked to pilot the Bill in Parliament. Ms Mamata Banerjee of the Trinamool Congress, an important partner in the coalition Government, revolted against the Bill. It had to be kept on the back burner because a shaky Congress could not stand against the opposition. The authorship of the Bill and the decision to keep it pending were solely attributed to Ms

Gandhi. The UPA Government did not receive any credit for such a socially progressive step. Second, the Congress party manifesto of 2009 Lok Sabha elections had made a commitment to make a law for food security of the poor. The Government and its experts including Mr Montek Ahluwalia's Planning Commission of India worked out a Bill on national food security. All hell broke loose when Ms Gandhi's NAC consisting of the 14 'wise men' rejected the Planning Commission's estimates of the BPL population in the country. Ms Gandhi pulled up the Government for messing up on such an important Bill. She instructed it to rework the food security Bill by re-estimating the number of poor in India. The Government revised its earlier estimate and the Bill given its assent by the Cabinet. Third, the Prevention of Communal Riot Bill has been pending from 2005 and had to be recast in 2009 because Ms Gandhi was not satisfied with the tone and tenor of the Bill.

The issue is not only about the existence of dual centres of power that have emerged during the rule of UPA. What is of concern here is that completely non-political individuals have been picked up for the NAC as conscience keepers of society. The Government of India and the State Governments have a highly evolved system of advisory bodies which suggest policies that are filtered by the Governments on the basis of political feasibility. In case of NAC there is no such filter. It is Ms Gandhi's wise men who are calling the shots and undermining democracy.

—1 July, 2010, The Pioneer

Negotiations could help End Insurgency

The Governments in the Maoist-affected States are at their wit's ends as they are unable to deal with the threat posed by Left-wing extremists who are officially identified as the 'greatest threat' to the internal security of the Indian state. It seems that the Congress-led UPA Government has been utterly confused in its response to the challenge of gun-wielding Left-wing extremists.

Prime Minister Manmohan Singh has always maintained that Maoism is a grave threat to peace and security of the country. But former Union Minister for Home Affairs Shivraj Patil, who had primary responsibility to maintain law and order, adopted a soft policy to deal with the Maoists. Later he was sacked for he also failed to face the challenge of terrorist attack in Mumbai on November 26, 2008.

In fact, it appears that the lack of political consensus within the political and governing apparatus has helped the Maoist expand their areas of operation. And as per the official-figure the number of Maoist-affected districts is set to increase from 83 to 100 out of total 626 districts in the country.

While addressing a meeting of the Director-Generals of police of nine Maoist-affected States on July 4, 2011, Union Minister for Home Affairs P Chidambaram announced an increase in the special security related expenditure for Maoist-affected districts. Mr Chidambaram also announced that 400 police stations in these States will be provided with sophisticated weapons. It has also been decided to launch strong police offensive against Maoists by providing 'helicopters and unmanned aerial vehicles' to liquidate Maoist menace.

In the meantime, Chief Minister of Odisha Naveen Patnaik asked the Home Minister to add four more districts to the already 15 districts under the security related expenditure scheme. Similarly, Chief Minister of Bihar Nitish Kumar, who during his first term openly differed with the Union Government's law and order approach to Left wing extremism and did not attend even the Chief Ministers' meeting, called for evolving a coordinated approach towards the problem at the meeting of Direction-Generals of police called by Mr Chidambaram. He asked the Centre 'to include five more district in the list of 15'.

However, the Communist Party of India and the Trinamool Congress don't agree either with the Union Government or Chief Ministers of Maoist-affected States that problem of Maoism can be tackled by following a 'law and order' approach. It is not only among the mainstream political parties, a large strata of intellectuals have serious differences of opinion among themselves about the genesis of the origin of Maoism from the 1970s and its continuous spread.

The Supreme Court judgement of July 5, 2011 that declares the anti-Maoist activities of Special Police Officers, popularly known as 'Salwa Judum' or 'Koya Commandos', of Chhattisgarh as illegal and unconstitutional is only one part of the verdict. The honourable judges said that "Indeed, we recognise that the state faces many serious problems on account of Maoist/Naxalite violence. Notwithstanding the fact that there may be social and economic circumstances, and certain policies followed by the State itself, leading to emergence of extremist violence, we cannot condone it."

The judges further observed "The attempt to overthrow the state itself and kill its agents, and perpetrate violence against innocent civilians, is destructive of an ordered life." The court has, in its very nuanced approach, made three observations that faulty public policies might have given birth to social discontent and cult of violence, it does not mean that violence, be condemned and state has an obligation to deal with Left wing extremism but it cannot 'out source' its own role to ill-educated and untrained 5,000 'foot soldier' in forest areas.

The Union Government has realised the limitations of 'law and order' approach and has sanctioned ₹ 25 crore each to 60 districts for schemes earmarked by a committee headed by district collector. The Government's special development scheme for 60 Maoist-affected areas is simple bureaucratic and centralised approach because local people should be involved in these schemes for which ₹ 25 crore has to be spent. The larger issue as has been highlighted by Maoist activities is that Maoists have been welcomed in States and districts which are generally tribal inhabited and mineral resources rich where foreign companies and multinationals have gone berserk in setting up their projects by uprooting the really poor and disempowered tribals.

The tribal population had traditional livelihood rights in forest and they made their living by selling forest products and local politicians, bureaucrats and contractors supported by the politicians of the State Government squeezed these poorest of the poor and in return earned huge profits by selling rich forest wealth. It is the duty of elected representatives to act as a buffer between the exploiter and the exploited especially the tribals who are most vulnerable sections of society. It deserves to be clearly asserted that Maoists have nothing in common with the theory and praxis of Karl Marx and their methods and agenda is completely deviant from the theory and praxis of Marxian 'class struggle'. Maoists are not leading a 'united conscious class movement' of the 'working and exploited rural and urban underclasses'. India Communist parties have always disowned Maoists both politically and ideologically.

Further, 'politics of gun' against the Indian state does not have any future prospects because not only elected Governments have popular and democratic legitimacy and mass support, the Armed Forces of the state are quite effective in dealing with violence of insurgency, terrorism, and Maoism. The so-called 'Liberation zones' of Maoists is a pipe dream and an utopia and by launching 'armed struggle' they have completely wrecked peaceful, democratic working class struggles for changing the social order.

Also, the state has a history of negotiations through mediators and interlocutors with gun-wielding insurgents in North-East and in Jammu and Kashmir. Many 'accords' have been signed between the functionaries of the Indian state and insurgents and conflicts have come to an end because the 'mediators' could bring the two opponent parties sit together for a negotiated settlement. Members of a 'moral brigade' should also be able to reach Maoists and help them arrive at a negotiated settlement with the state.

—12 July, 2010, The Pioneer

Congress has Betrayed its Ideals

The Congress party has dominated the Indian political landscape and it truly deserves its moniker of the Grand Old Party of India. The party has remained in the summit of power because it once successfully led the country on the basis of its distinct, even distinctive, socio-economic and political agenda.

It is a well established fact that parties in a competitive democracy contest on the basis of their own agendas and voters make their choices by supporting or opposing agendas presented by different parties on the eve of elections. What is the performance record of the Congress-in-Government in its seventh year of managing the affairs of the country?

Does the Congress have any distinctive sociocultural and political agenda except the liberalisation and privatisation of Indian economy? The most important agenda of the Congress has historically been the modernisation of society through democratic methods. But today the Congress has not only abandoned its essential agenda of social modernisation but it is playing a reactionary and socially regressive role while dealing with important issues.

All-India Congress Committee president Sonia Gandhi claims to be a great protector of women rights and gender equality, yet she and her party has completely refused to play any activist role against the cruelty meted out by the Jat-Gujjar dominated *khaps* which are violating every law of the land in the States of Rajasthan, Haryana and Uttar Pradesh. The Congress-led State Governments here have given full licence to the panchayats to act as a 'State within a State' and pronounce judgements which are in the domain of established courts of law.

The worst culprits in this regard have been Haryana Chief Minister Bhupinder Singh Hooda and two MPs, Mr Deepender Hooda and Mr Navin Jindal, who jointly form the 'modern face' of the Congress from the State. The trio is carrying on its shoulders the burden of legitimising the *khaps'* notorious atrocities. Leaders of the Jat and Gujjar communities have been encouraged to demand legal recognition for the *khaps* and also an amendment of the Hindu Marriage Act. Union Ministers Mr Kamal Nath,

Mr Kapil Sibal and Mr MS Gill have also expressed serious reservations on the issue of Government action against *khaps.* A proposal on bringing to book the crime of abetment of 'honour killings' brought by the Union Government under pressure to act on the matter has been referred to a Group of Ministers as a time-wasting measure. In the light of this narrative, it is impossible to imagine that Ms Gandhi has any convictions regarding the women's reservation Bill which is lying in cold storage owing to vacillations by the Congress leadership.

A ruling party not only leads the country on the basis of its own agenda but also accommodates parts of the agenda of Opposition parties that are in tune with its own ideology. Former Prime Minister Jawaharlal Nehru always 'stole' important ideas of the Opposition parties. Nehru never allowed any Opposition party to raise the flag of Socialism because he presented himself as a better champion of Socialist ideals. Mrs Indira Gandhi, whose only commitment was to remain in power at all costs, was able to steal a march over her opponents by projecting herself, rightly or otherwise, as a "protector of the poor" in India. However, the present Congress leadership is in no position to appropriate the progressive agenda of Opposition parties.

After the Supreme Court upheld the Bombay High Court's lifting of ban on a book on Maratha leader Shivaji, Maharashtra's Congress party Chief Minister Ashok Chavan joined issue with the Shiv Sena and prohibited sale of the book in the State. Is Ms Gandhi not capable of defending the basic values of democracy? Why should Mr Chavan not hand over power to Shiv Sena if he has no alternative political value system to uphold as Chief Minister of the State?

The same story is repeated by the Congress on the issue of the dispute between Maharashtra and Karnataka on Belgaum. The all-India vision of the Congress has collapsed under the threat of the movement launched by Telangana Rashtriya Samiti. What is the utility of appointing the Justice Srikrishna Committee to study the demand for Telangana unless the Congress has lost its capacity to decide on a purely political issue like the creation of a new State?

The Janata Party emerged with great fanfare in 1977 but ended up in fragments because of casteism and also because it did not have a cohesive ideology of its own. Caste in politics or narrow regionalism cannot be a substitute for the project of modernity of India which has been the hallmark of Congress. But the Congress party organisation is pursuing its own goals and interests at the State level. Perhaps, the late YS Rajasekhara Reddy's son, Mr YS Jaganmohan Reddy, cannot be faulted for pursuing his own agenda of winning the Chief Minister's chair in Andhra Pradesh only because the Congress has no ideology except self-promotion and dynasty politics.

—20 July, 2010, The Pioneer

Why Democrats should Worry

The Indian state inherited a developed, well-knit and organized coercive infrastructure from the retreating colonial state—highly-disciplined armed and police forces and a 'steel frame' bureaucracy. The government of independent India not only made full use of this inherited military and police apparatus for managing the crisis created by the transfer of population post Partition, it also used its military power in a war against Pakistan in the state of Jammu and Kashmir and in the operations against the Nizam of Hyderabad and the Communist-led armed struggle in the Telengana region. The extraordinary events of 1947-48 not only legitimatized the men in uniform in the estimation of a democratically elected government, they also strengthened the argument that the British had left behind extremely useful instruments of coercive power for the successor rulers who in turn used it effectively for the maintenance of internal and external security.

Unlike the unaccountable and undemocratic colonial rulers, a real challenge before the political leaders of independent India was how to establish a proper institutional relationship between 'democracy and military and police forces'. Clearly, the role and authority which the British commander-in-chief exercised in the governance of colonial India as an unquestioned head of the armed forces was not acceptable under a democratic political system. Our political leadership resolved this issue by drawing upon the fundamental traditions of British and American democracies and locating control of the coercive machinery in the hands of democratically elected leaders. Yet, the developments of the last sixty years also provides enough evidence that not only has the manifest and latent authority of the Indian Army and police forces increased in public life, the actual dependence of civil democratic authority on 'soldiers' for the maintenance of internal security has undergone substantial change. The days of ordinary policing for the maintenance of routine law and order seem to have come to an end and elected governments, both at the Centre and the state levels, have substantially handed over the management of problems of internal security to army-trained police forces.

A cataloguing of specialized and armed police forces established by the central government will reveal that dependence of our political governing class over such forces has increased because the central and state governments are unable, even incapable, of dealing with internal social discontent and group violence. The Border Security Force established in 1965 now has 2,19,560 personnel. The Central Industrial Security Force, a specialized armed police for the protection of industrial undertakings created in 1969 today has 1,20,000 personnel. The Crown Representative Police, renamed after independence as the Central Reserve Police Force, today consists of 206 battalions handling a wide range of duties covering law and order and counter-insurgency, anti-militancy and anti-terrorism operations. The force plays a key role in assisting states in maintaining public order and countering subversive activities of militant groups, not only in J&K and the Northeast but also the Maoist affected regions in central India. The central government also deploys Rapid Action Force (1992), the Commando Battalions for Resolute Action (COBRA), Indo-Tibetan Border Force, National Security Guard, Sashastra Seema Bal (2001) and the Railway Protection Force and the Railway Police.

Our democratically-elected Parliament has not only extended full support to the creation of powerful militarized police forces for internal security, it has also approved draconian laws for the unlimited exercise of coercive powers by these forces. The Armed Forces Special Powers Act (AFSPA) enacted on 11 September 1958 states: The Centre or state government can notify 'an area as disturbed under AFPSA and invoke the Act and powers are given to the army, central paramilitary forces, including even junior non-commissioned officers to (*a*) fire or use force even causing death, (*b*) destroy any structure, (*c*) arrest any person without a warrant and (*d*) search any person without a warrant.' In the exercise of powers conferred under AFPSA, 'No prosecution can be launched without the approval of the Centre.' The states of Jammu and Kashmir as also northeast India, especially Manipur and Nagaland, are not only controlled by the armed forces along with the democratically elected state governments, they are governed by a super-coercive law like AFSPA. Our Parliament has thus legitimatized the extraordinary coercive powers which are exercised by the army and police functionaries over the rights and liberties of citizens under the broad rubric of national interest, security and integrity of the country. It is worth recollecting that Indira Gandhi's emergency regime with its suspension of habeas corpus was sought to be given a legal veneer under the provisions of the constitution of a democratic Republic of India.

Further, post-independence India launched its democratic journey by placing 'draconian' laws on the statute book which provided ample powers to police forces who could 'detain' any citizen, sacrificing the rights and liberties of ordinary individuals at the altar of the defence of the state. Our democratic state has always felt a need to create of specialized and well-equipped militarized forces on the plea that anti-insurgency, or anti-naxalism, or anti-terrorism are national threats and they require an extraordinary response. Post the terrorist attack on Mumbai on 26 November 2008, the Indian state sought to strengthen its military and legal capabilities by creating a National Security Agency and enacting fresh anti-terrorism laws. Incidentally, every state government too has extraordinary laws to place any individual behind bars without the right of trial.

What is the explanation for the growing involvement of coercive police forces in internal law and order issues? Why have the democratically elected governments, whether at the Centre or the state levels, come to depend on the assistance of paramilitary police forces and draconian laws infringing on the rights and freedoms of citizens? Why has Parliament willingly sanctioned extraordinary coercive powers to the political executive for performing its basic and routine functioning of governance based on constitutional values of freedom of citizens? What is the rationale for a democratic government to enact a Preventive Detention Act, Maintenance of Internal Security Act, Prevention of Terrorist Activities Act and other anti-terrorism laws?

Prime Minister Manmohan Singh and the Home Minister P. Chidambaram have repeatedly maintained that 'Naxalism is the greatest threat to internal security', while forgetting that these misguided armed Maoist adventurists are completely 'home grown' and a product of the social soil of India. True, the accumulated social discontent of the tribals is exploited by the Maoists, but the 'real' creators and originators of social turmoil of the tribal belt are the functionaries of the Indian state who have always neglected their problems. In the same manner, many identity-based armed struggles in Northeast India are the result of real or imaginary grievances of the people living in the remote parts of the country. Is military operation the answer? It is a well-known fact that uniform wearing armed forces are deployed when democrats fail to feel the real pulse of the people and redress their grievances. This is the reality.

It is often pointed out that our armed and para-military forces operate under the democratic-political control of elected representatives. This, however, is only one face of Indian democracy. Behind this mask of democratic control over 'soldiers' lies the other reality of the growing indispensability of armed forces to manage the internal affairs on the basis of coercion. If over 150 districts are Naxal infested and Northeastern Indian states and Jammu and Kashmir are classified as 'disturbed' states, democratically elected representatives must look within because soldiers out of barracks have tilted the power balance in their favour. The Indian situation proves that democracies become weak when disgruntled social groups come out on the streets and armed forces are deployed to crush the people's movements. Democrats should be worried.

—July, 2010, Seminar 611

Deviant Regionalism Swamps UPA

Provisions of the Indian Constitution have very clearly and comprehensively provided the Centre with more than enough powers to direct, guide and supervise the State Governments in performing their duties and obligations by keeping in mind national goals and national interests. But, in the last 60 years, by taking refuge behind constitutional provisions, the Union Government has completely misused its powers, especially while dealing with State Governments ruled by Opposition parties.

Every Government at the Centre, irrespective of the party or coalition of parties in power, has engaged itself with State Governments, irrespective of the party or coalition in power on crucial issues concerning national interests. Hence the incumbent Government cannot pretend it is unable to ensure that State Governments implement national policies decided by the Parliament.

However, the Manmohan Singh Government has completely failed to deal effectively with serious political deviations by some of the State Governments and leaders of the regional parties while implementing national policies. The most important failure has been observed in implementing a coherent policy framework while dealing with the problematic Maoist issue. Union Home Minister P Chidambaram has repeatedly been conveying the message that "Maoist terrorism has become a great challenge before the security forces of this country" but in spite of making every effort to arrive at a consensus with the Chief Ministers of Maoist-affected States, the Union Government has completely failed to involve them in implementing any coherent and well-coordinated all-India policy to deal with the scourge.

The Chief Minister of Bihar, Mr Nitish Kumar, has made it a point to keep himself absent from the meetings of Chief Ministers convened by the Centre to evolve a common policy to deal with Maoism. Not only this but, alongwith RJD chief Lalu Prasad, he has publicly stated that the Centre's policy of 'bullet versus bullet' is counterproductive because Maoism is a 'social and economic problem' and a 'product of the backwardness which prevails in these States'. Further, Mr Shibu Soren, a charismatic leader and former Chief Minister of Jharkhand, another State under Maoist attack, has not only been soft-pedaling the problem of Maoism but has taken full support from Maoist cadre to win seats for his party during the State Assembly elections.

The story does not end here. Manipur remained cut off for more than 60 days because national highways 39 and 53—the lifelines of the State—were blocked by protesting Naga youth. The Centre remained a helpless spectator while the people of Manipur suffered hardships because trucks carrying essential supplies could not enter the State. The Union Government did not issue a clear directive that police forces of every neighbouring State Government in the North-east region should assist the Manipur Government to clear the blockade. This has encouraged Naga bodies to re-impose a 20-day blockade in the region. Sikkim has also been victim of such a blockade by Gorkhaland agitators and neither the Centre nor the State Government of West Bengal thought it fit to put in a coordinated effort to get it removed. The Union Government is completely incapable of motivating the concerned State Governments on the matter or even assure them that, if need be, the Centre will immediately dispatch security forces to assist them in their task.

This brings us to the situation in the Kashmir Valley. Groups of stone-pelters are on a rampage here and, despite the best efforts of Chief Minister Omar Abdullah and Mr Chidambaram, political parties which participate in the electoral process in Jammu and Kashmir have refused to evolve an all-party consensus on the issue of restoration of law and order in the Valley. It deserves to be mentioned that even Syed Ali Shah Geelani, who is a separatist leader, appealed to the stone-throwing groups to stop their activity and his voice was heeded by the agitators. But Mufti Mohammad Sayeed's People's Democratic Party has refused to play any role in the matter. How can Ms Mehbooba Mufti and her father, who have enjoyed the benefits of democracy and held high offices in elected Governments such as those of Union Home Minister and Chief Minister, refuse to participate in consensus making initiatives taken by Mr Abdullah or the Prime Minister's all-party conference on August 10? Separatists like Mr Geelani or Mr Sajjad Lone are identifiable but the duplicity of the Mufti family is tolerated only by a spineless Union Government.

Political initiatives in Jammu and Kashmir led to the launch of the Samjhauta Express and the Karwan-e-Aman for 'divided families' on both sides of the border. Kashmir needs a healing touch and the Centre must adopt a stick-and-carrot policy to deal with many problems but such an approach has not been successfully implemented by the UPA Government. If Ms Mamata Banerjee, who is a Railway Minister in the Manmohan Singh Government, can openly associate with Maoists, described by her own Government as the most important threat to national security, and organise a political rally in West Bengal's Lalgarh with the active and open support of the Maoists, it is futile to expect any leadership by the Centre in the disturbed States of West Bengal and Jammu and Kashmir.

— 24 August, 2010, The Pioneer

Through CWG We Fail Gandhi

Rupert Emerson, the famous American political scientist, stated in his seminal and path-breaking book, *Empire to Nation: the Decolonisation Process,* that there were two models of struggle against colonial rule in Asia and Africa. One model was personified in Mao and the other in Mahatma Gandhi. Both influenced the leadership of their times, but the everlasting contribution was of Gandhi. Nelson Mandela, a product of anti-colonial struggles, is known as the "Gandhi of South Africa" because he embraced the great leader's style of protest.

The 19th Commonwealth Games will open in New Delhi on October 3, a day after Mahatma Gandhi's 141st birth anniversary. The most striking aspect of all the scandal and shame of the Commonwealth Games is the open display of anti-Gandhism by India's ruling elite comprising all the mainstream political parties, the bureaucracy and the compliant media, which despite highlighting the scam, is not questioning the fundamentals. A Maoist leader from deep in the jungles of Orissa can be credited with true patriotism for objecting to the "Queen's Baton" in independent India. Mahatma Gandhi lived for the freedom of India. But the Commonwealth Games celebrates something which the father of our nation deemed shameful: India's slavery under the British.

The overarching consensus seems to be: forget the corruption till the Games are over—national pride will be hurt otherwise. This defies logic. The vast majority of Indians would point out that it is far more shameful to have schools without roofs, hospitals without doctors and starving tribals being stripped of the last vestiges of their pride by land-grabbing industrialists. Why should national pride today be sought through displaying stadia and swimming pools? Isn't India's contribution to the development of architecture since ancient times already known? The irony of the whole situation is that national pride is being measured in terms of one very limited activity like CWG. India has a history of great achievements in the field of art, architecture, discoveries in the sciences. India's self confidence stems from our heritage that shows that we can achieve the impossible even under impossible conditions.

Nationalism can be used very positively for achieving grand vision and dreams. It can also be misused to bring wars and disasters. Mussolini's statist nationalism and Hitler's pride in the German race. BJP wanted to emulate its fascist hero, Hitler, in organising the CWG just as the Nazi dictator organised the Olympic Games in 1933. As a student, I was shown Hitler's picture lording over the Olympic crowd. The only difference now is that while Hitler could at least boast of a success, all that modern India can manage to show as "achievement" are a few hopeless stadia with leaky roofs and damaged floors.

The purpose of the reference to Gandhi is to tell the Indians of this generation that it is not only the earlier generation but everybody who cared for the glorious history of struggle for Independence is proud of Gandhi. Indians have a feeling which is very legitimate that we belong to the country of Gandhi. This rich legacy of great pride is lying in a shambles, fully wrecked by scandals and immorality of the actions of the organisers of the Commonwealth Games.

The Indian leadership keeps on shouting from housetops that India is a country in the 21st century and the media, both print and audio-visual in India and important Commonwealth countries like Britain and Australia, are carrying headlines that the organisers of the Games have 'eaten away' all public and private funds which were meant for the event. Every individual on the streets of Delhi is talking about the rampant corruption in the ongoing, indecent hurry to complete the construction work.

Is this the India of Gandhi? It is strange that the Prime Minister, who is overall incharge of the project, woke up from his slumber so late. He took the strange step of asking his Cabinet Secretary to take bureaucratic control of the organisation at the last minute. Manmohan Singh has depicted himself as the modern-day version of Kumbhakarna, the mythical brother of Ravana in Ramayana, who was blissfully unaware of the large-scale loot that went on in the name of organising the Games.

—28 August, 2010, The Pioneer

In Pursuit of Good Governance

The beginning of 1990 is like a watershed in the political and economic journey of India when America, which had emerged as the sole economic and military superpower, succeeded in selling to the Indians its own ideology of free-market economy and Indians opted for American model of economic development by abandoning its own model of self-reliance for planned economic development.

Indian ideologues of free-market economy, following in the footsteps of the western capitalist country, opted for complete integration with the global capitalist system and Indian market was opened for flow of western finance capital and free trade with capitalist countries.

The western multinational corporations were welcomed to India to make financial investments in the Indian market. Western financial investors found a very hospitable political climate and at the same time they experienced many administrative hurdles and bottlenecks while doing business in India. This new situation, which had emerged due to the "opening" of Indian economy to western capitalist class, brought World Bank, International Monetary Fund, Rockefeller Foundation, Ford Foundation, Brookings Institution and Centre for Democracy and Governance funded by speculator billionaire George Soros, who sold the agenda of good governance to Indian politicians, public policymakers and university based client academics not only to study the existing causes of inefficiencies and delays caused by administrators but also suggest ways and means to improve administrative practices

with a view to facilitate the arrival of foreign finance capital.

All above-mentioned American controlled and funded organisations not only sold the agenda of improvement of governance, they also prioritised and cataloged the main areas which required a deep study by hired and funded client academics and the government of India to set its own house in order. All these above-mentioned American funded agencies at the Western corporate class and financial investors identified (a) corruption (b) centralisation as the main roadblocks in the way of speedy decision-making by the governments, both at the Centre and at the state levels of

India. The government of India has appointed a high-powered Administrative Reform Committee under the chairmanship of its Law minister Veerappa Moily and Moily Commission has submitted many reports for administrative reforms to the government of India. The so-called autonomous academic and quasi-academic institutions have also been funded by foreign agencies to undertake studies concerning the plague of corruption in public institutions and also suggest ways and means for the 'decentralisation' of public decision-making instead of the present obsolete system of centralisation of governmental decision-making machinery in India.

It deserves to be clearly stated that improvement and reform of the infected colonial state apparatus with a view to bring governance in tune with the new demands of the democratic form of government of India after Independence. Jawaharlal Nehru Model of economic planning required community participation and involvement of the people at the grassroot levels in rural India. Nehru in 1950s and 1960s focused his attention on community development and decentralisation of decision-making by empowering village, Taluka and district-level Panchayati Raj. It is during the era of planned economic development that the Nehru government established the Balwant Rai Mehta Committee on Panchayati Raj and on the basis of this very important committee, the state governments, especially of Rajasthan, Gujarat and Maharashtra, launched the grand experiment of Panchayati Raj in the early 1960s. This thread was taken further by Rajiv Gandhi (1984-1989) when he brought a very forward looking Bill on Panchayati Raj which was unfortunately defeated in the Rajya Sabha. Rajiv's successor PV Narasimha Rao in 1991 successfully piloted the Panchayati Raj Bill and a big experiment of decentralisation of power, up to the grassroot level, was launched in India without waiting for the advice of western funded givers for such a project. The real intention of the multinational corporations and western finance capital investors is not to encourage decentralisation of power up to Panchayat level, but to erode or weaken the authority of the Central government for the regulation of economy even under free market model. The real villain of the piece is the Central government and the proxy agenda sold by these western funds givers is a demand for decentralisation of power. Imagine, if the Centre had no power to direct, guide and supervise smallest operations, the multinationals would have a free hand in investments by violating all norms of environmental considerations.

Western multinationals are keen to operate in India because they want to escape regulatory environmental laws from their country and enjoy the 'free for all' atmosphere in India. President Obama strictly dealt with British Petroleum when it allowed oil leak but poor Indians died and Anderson, chief of the Union Carbide plant, went scot-free and flew to his country after killing thousands of Indians.

Hence, the slogan of anti-centralisers masquerading as promoters of good governance is detrimental to the authority of the Central government. Indians have been grappling with the plague of corruption in public decision-making and even before so-called expert academic institutions for the study of governance were established by American fund-giving foundations, Central and state vigilance commissions, Lokpals and Lokayukts were established to investigate and launch prosecution against public functionaries involved in corruption. The Right to Information Act and the state and Central information commissioners have further 'opened' up the working of secretive government, and public accountability of public decision-makers has been ensured. Did Indians wait to get wisdom for Right to Information law from American-funded institutions for the study of governance? Corruption in India has increased by leaps and bounds after the "opening up of the Indian economy" to western multinationals and finance capital investors. Americans should be told: Physician, heal thyself! The Indian ambassador to the United States recently informed the government of India that powerful American companies had paid hefty bribes to some important Indian companies including some public sector industries.

The above narrative clearly shows that the focus on good governance has been reduced by foreign fund-giving foundations to trivialities like improvement in procedures and techniques of public decision-making. It is essential to demystify the foreign exported agenda of good governance because it is a demand of western finance capital investors to make governance investor-friendly and for that abandon the so-called legal framework for the protection of the mineral wealth of India and it should be substituted by speedy decision-making in favour of freedom for investors.

The central issue which has been evaded and avoided is that the slogan of good governance is quite secondary because politics is the prime mover of all crucial and critical economic decisions in every society including India. The western financial investors and donor agencies for academic research have pushed the agenda of critical enquiry about political power and replaced it by a non-controversial public discourse on improvement of governance. Is it a political question or an issue of good governance if social inequality is increasing under the new regime of liberalisation, privatisation and globalisation? Will corruption- free, decentralized and real federal Panchayati Raj based governance eradicate or perpetuate gross social inequalities? The mega-issue of income disparities, exclusion of the majority of Indian population from the benefits of economic growth and disempowerment of the labouring classes under the present regime demand serious discussion on the ideology of politics pursued by the Indians beginning from the 1990s, and instead of discussion on politics, the focus has shifted towards peripheral issues of good governance based on efficient methods of work by the administrators.

—21 August, 2010, Sahara Time

Playing the Messiah of the Dispossessed

Mamata's perceived proximity to Maoists and her failure to offer an ideological alternative are alarming, writes CP Bhambhri

Obituaries have been written in the mass media about Mr Buddhadeb Bhattacharjee's Left Front Government in West Bengal. The mass media has not only prematurely predicted the electoral demise of the Left Front Government but has also decided that Ms Mamata Banerjee's Trinamool Congress would emerge winner. The turning point in this anti-Left political and intellectual tirade took place with the police firing in Singur where land had been acquired for the Tata small car project. Singur and later Nandigram became a symbol of the 'anti-farmer' policies of the Left Front Government and without going into the mental and political make-up of Ms Banerjee, she was declared by all anti-Left forces in the State and the country as their 'saviour' from Communist misrule. It is ironical that Ratan Tata made a public statement that his business competitors and opponents were supporting Ms Banerjee's agitation against the proposed small car project. That her supporters did not react adversely to such a grave allegation by Mr Tata whom the mass media has always projected as a model Indian industrialist is also significant.

The worst was yet to come. In a rally in Lalgarh on August 9 Ms Banerjee publicly acknowledged the support of Maoists in her campaign to dislodge the Left Front Government. Ms Banerjee's open affection towards the Maoists in West Bengal was further substantiated when she announced that Maoist leader Azad had been 'murdered' by security forces. Ms Banerjee was not asked a simple question about her favourable pronouncements even though the Prime Minister, Mr Manmohan Singh, and Home Minister P Chidambaram have been shouting down from the rooftops that the Maoists comprise the greatest security threat to India. It is clear that Mr Singh and Ms Banerjee are not sailing in the same boat on the issue of the Maoist threat to the nation's security. Mr Chidambaram has described Azad's death as the result of a genuine encounter with security forces while Ms Banerjee described it as murder and both cannot be right. Evidently, a coalition partner of the Union Government is openly dissociating itself from its views and policies. The Parliament wanted an explanation from Ms Banerjee about her positive statements on the Maoists especially in the context of her being Union Minister for Railways. She decided to stay put in Kolkata and Finance Minister Pranab Mukherjee came out in defence of her statement. Mr Mukherjee went to the extent of saying that the Government knew about her views on Naxalism.

The Naxalite movement began from Naxalbari in West Bengal and the Congress Government led by Chief Minister Siddhartha Shankar Ray suppressed it brutally. The land reform policies initiated by the Left Front Government that succeeded Mr Ray's Government in 1977 helped pacify the disgruntled peasantry to a large extent. Of late, Naxalism has again emerged in West Bengal and Lalgarh is the headquarters of this armed struggle. Is Ms Banerjee consciously or unconsciously not helping in the revival of the Naxal movement in West Bengal by accepting their support against the Left Front Government?

A brief political profile of Ms Banerjee deserves to be mentioned here. Critics of the Left Front Government and the Communist movement in West Bengal have repeatedly alleged that the CPI(M) cadre consists of lumpen elements, criminals and extortionists. Such an allegation can be also leveled against Ms Banerjee's supporters. Many young deideologised street fighters are moving towards her as they see her as the rising star of Bengal politics. Should the country not be worried about a future Chief Minister who is providing shelter to young street fighters? It is a well-known fact that Ms Banerjee's politics is completely non-ideological and opportunistic. She had no hesitation in joining the Ministry of the Atal Bihari Vajpayee-led NDA Government and because of her temperamental behaviour had to quit her portfolio. She has shown her ideological bankruptcy by joining the UPA2 Government. It can be legitimately asked what kind of political and ideological alternative Ms Banerjee is capable of offering the people of West Bengal.

Public memory is proverbially short but her performance as Railway Minister for the year 2009-10 is before the enquiring public. Her only interest now is to dislodge the Left Front Government in West Bengal and occupy the Chief Minister's chair. But West Bengal deserves a better leader than the temperamental, immature, unprincipled and opportunistic Ms Banerjee. She has no alternative programme to offer to the people of the State.

It is nobody's case that, in a parliamentary democracy, a single party or coalition of parties permanently rule a country or a State. Hence a change of power in West Bengal is most acceptable. The real worrisome issue is the model of politics which will be pursued by Ms Banerjee if she wins the forthcoming State Assembly elections. Ms Banerjee exhibits all tendencies of a populist leader and is given to unpredictable moves and political gimmicks. The people of West Bengal have a right to know the role which the gun-wielding Maoists will play under her patronage. The whole country is worried about Ms Banerjee and her politics at the Centre and the State. Although she is being projected as a messiah by her supporters, her leadership may plunge West Bengal into anarchy.

—7 September, 2010, The Pioneer

Manmohan Singh must Clarify Stand to Party

The Prime Minister's public statements and pronouncements deserve to be taken very seriously not least because the implications of the speech of any head of political executive in a democracy have a great deal of import.

Besides, Mr Manmohan Singh, who leads a difficult coalition, needs to clarify his political standing within his own party from time to time. An impression of leadership deficit exists in the public mind and this is another reason why his statements assume more significance. Perhaps, if Ms Sonia Gandhi were president of Congress rather than also the United Progressive Alliance chairperson, Mr Singh's authority would have been seen as less disputed.

In a meeting with select editors on September 6, Mr Singh, therefore, divided his utterances into two parts—the first a declaration of his own status as Prime Minister and his standing in the Council of Ministers and the second a statement on important public policy priorities and challenges faced by his Government and the country.

It deserves to be clearly stated that as the chosen and official nominee of Ms Gandhi it is imperative for Mr Singh to convey to the whole country that he is safe in his seat of power. Ms Gandhi reserves the right to nominate Pradesh Congress Committee presidents and other functionaries of her party including Mr Singh who knows full well that there are many contenders for the post of Prime Minister.

Former Minister for External Affairs Natwar Singh frequently claimed direct access to Ms Gandhi on the basis of his proximity to Mrs Indira Gandhi and Rajiv Gandhi. Mr Natwar Singh claimed foreign policy was solely in his domain and the Prime Minister's Office had nothing to do with it and that he enjoyed special status in the Government. Old warhorse Arjun Singh never tired of reminding Ms Gandhi that it was he, along with Mr Narayan Dutt Tiwari, who helped Ms Gandhi establish a hold in politics. How could such a 'loyalist' be ignored and an 'outsider' brought in to head the Government led by the Congress?

A demand was also raised for creation of the post of Deputy Prime Minister. The not-so-subtle message was that Mr Singh's wings be clipped.

Ms Gandhi publicly dismissed the idea of 'special loyalists' and Deputy Prime Ministership during UPA's tenure of 2004-2009. The machinations of factional heavyweights in the Congress continued despite the dishonourable exits of Mr Natwar Singh and Mr Arjun Singh from the Cabinet and the idea of bringing Mr Rahul Gandhi into the Cabinet was pursued. Mr Singh is intelligent enough never to claim that he is taller than a Nehru or an Indira and, by citing the right examples, nipped in the bud schemes of those who had aspirations tied to the creation of the post.

His assertion of cohesiveness in the Council of Ministers is, however, off the mark. Every coalition partner exercises his or her 'veto' to Cabinet proposals not acceptable to it as witnessed in Trinamool Congress' opposition to the Land Acquisition (Amendment) Bill and Mr M. Karunanidhi's role in Mr A. Raja's continuance as Union Minister.

The second and more important part of the Prime Minister's pronouncements on September 6 include his observations on the Maoist crisis and India's policy towards Pakistan. Also, for the first time, he warned the nation about a growing threat from China. It is the duty of a Prime Minister to frequently take public opinion into confidence because, in a democracy, political leaders have to inform, even educate, the citizens on critical issues.

On the Maoist issue, Prime Minister stated unambiguously that "there are no quick fixes". He observed that for tackling the problem "valid economic and social issues have to be addressed but law and order has also to be enforced". The Prime Minister also defended Home Minister P Chidambaram's handling of the matter. This assumes great importance in the light of veteran leader Digvijay Singh's differences with Mr Chidambaram.

Mr Singh stated that the "lines of communication" with Pakistan must be kept open irrespective of complexities in Kashmir. The UPA Government's policy towards Pakistan is well-known but it is for the first time that the Prime Minister has stated that "China wants India to be in state of low-level equilibrium". He chose to bring out areas of Sino-Indian conflict in public. "China would like to have a foothold in South Asia and we have to reflect this reality. We have to be aware of this," he clearly said.

A week later, while addressing the Combined Commanders Conference that included the three Service Chiefs with Defence Minister AK Antony on September 13, he referred to "China improving its military and physical infrastructure". Mr Antony went a step further and stated that "in fact, there has been an increasing assertiveness on the part of China". The Prime Minister contextualised it by stating that "the fact is that we cannot realise our growth ambitions unless we ensure peace and stability in South Asia. The countries of the Gulf, West Asia and Central Asia are our natural partners".

The Prime Minister's meetings of September 6 and 12 are to be analysed as one whole framework of his thinking, leaving aside his battles within the Congress. Coalition partners in the UPA and all Opposition parties should focus their attention on the Maoist problem, Pakistan and China and put the Prime Minister under scrutiny on these subjects. Has he been able to provide leadership in resolving these contentious issues or offer some alternative lines of policy in the national interest?

—22 September, 2010, The Pioneer

Congress Non-ideological Pragmatism

Rahul Gandhi has been projected by the media as the messiah of the poor, downtrodden Dalits, tribals and farmers. Rahul started his political journey by staying at the huts of poor Dalit families and sharing their frugal meals. Mayawati, in particular, was vocal in her criticism of Rahuls antics because she considers herself the sole custodian of Dalit interests. However, Rahul managed to convey the message that it is not Mayawati but he, along with his mother, who is the real protector and defender of Dalit rights. Rahul went on to visit villages and houses of poor and exploited tribals whose rights to natural wealth were being snatched by multinationals and big industrial houses. On August 26, Rahul congratulated ancient Dongria Kondh on their victory... by succeeding in halting the Vedanta bid to mine bauxite in the Niyamgiri hills of Orissa.

Rahul championed the cause of poor tribals in their fight against exploiters who, under the garb of industrial development, were trampling on their rights. Many political leaders perceive the ongoing Maoist insurgency against the Indian state as the last-ditch attempt by the exploited tribals of Chhattisgarh, Jharkhand, Orissa, etc, to preserve their rights. It is true that in many places, tribals consider the Maoists as their liberators. But Rahul has accepted the Maoist challenge head-on by reaching out to the tribals to assure them of protection of their rights.

Speaking at a rally at Jagannathpur in Kalahandhi district of Orissa on August 26, Rahul told the tribals that development did not mean ignoring the genuine voices of people. His rhetoric has alarmed votaries of development because the Vedanta project was seen as a symbol of industrialisation in Orissa.

Going further, Rahul has also voiced his concern at the appropriation of land from farmers by big business houses to set up industries and malls. For Rahul, the opportunity knocked when the fertile Green Revolution belt in western Uttar Pradesh was gripped by an agitation by farmers whose land had been acquired by the Mayawati government to construct the Greater Noida-Yamuna Expressway. Rahul led a delegation of UP farmers to Delhi and met the PM, who assured the farmers that their lands would be fully protected.

Rahuls pro-poor, pro-Dalit, pro-tribal and pro-farmer politics was supported by Sonia Gandhi who made a statement amplifying the concerns raised by Rahul. On September 9, she declared: Land acquisition must be done in a way that fertile lands are not lost. Farmers should be provided adequate compensation. The UPA government is ready to bring the Land Acquisition (Amendment) Act, 2010.

It is clear from the approach of the Congress top leadership that it is absolutely committed to the project of growth and economic development that is integrally linked to industrialisation and private foreign investment and harnessing new technologies. Both Sonia, as chairperson of the UPA, and Rahul, as the general secretary of the Congress, have led from the front to highlight the partys new line of growth with a human face.

The statements of Rahul and Sonia, along with the Supreme Courts concern for the informal sector of economy, including the welfare of construction workers, can lead to an impression that the Congress is abandoning the path of development that it chose in the 1990s and replacing it with the old system of leftofcentre policies pursued by the party under Indira Gandhi. Have Rahul or Sonia given any impression that they are reverting to the old ideology of socialism A caring state that protects the rights of the oppressed and exploited sections of society and practises social welfare policies cannot be described as a socialist system.

THE history of how industrialising capitalist countries of the West dealt with the issue of rights of citizens clearly shows that industrial capitalist societies gradually brought the discourse of the rights of the labouring class within their policy framework. Thomas Paine wrote in his classic Rights of Man in 1791 that both the American War of Independence and the French Revolution were based on the idea of the fundamental right to freedom and equality.

The last decades of the 18th century and the whole 19th and 20th centuries have witnessed working class struggles for rights and their powerful impact was felt on the industrial capitalist classes and the policymaking apparatus of western countries. The enlightened self-interest of the employers became the central point while they were dealing with workers for enhancement of productivity and profits. As a result, the idea of welfare state spread in the whole of Europe. The Green Party of Germany, for example, espouses concern for the environment and ecology but its ideology has not acted as an obstacle in the way of capitalist growth of the country. The Scandanavian countries of Sweden, Norway, Denmark and Finland are strong democratic welfare state traditions. But it has in no way adversely affected profits and productivity of western capitalism.

There is no disconnect between social welfare market economics of Europe and their economic growth trajectory because every social class and group, on the basis of historical experience of industrialisation, has come to realise that a politics that seek to primarily uphold working class interests has to be guided by a pragmatic definition of enlightened self-interest. Hence, European welfare capital is not at all guided by any ideology of socialism because experience has shown that non-ideological pragmatism is a good guide to diffuse social conflicts which arise if the labouring classes are neglected and they are not provided with social security. The message of Thomas Paine has been imbibed by major industrial capital societies.

It appears that Rahul and Sonia have learnt their lessons from European history that capitalism will not be subverted by taking care of the concerns and rights of the socially downtrodden classes. The path they want to follow is based not on any ideology or doctrine but on the pragmatist considerations of promoting social welfare of the poor. They have not abandoned centrist politics. On the contrary, they have just given a pragmatic touch to governance.

—25 September, 2010, The Economic Times

Faith and Belief cannot be Given Veto Power Over Rule of Law

An extremely worrisome and highly controversial principle has been asserted by the Allahabad High Court while deciding the Ayodhya title suits. The judges asserted that matters of 'faith and belief' have an absolute veto power over the 'fact and legality of the ownership of mosque or temple under the dispute.'

An analysis of the judgment requires reference to Articles 25 and 26 of the Constitution on the Right to Freedom of Religion, the right to manage religious affairs and relevant judicial verdicts, for example, cited by PM Bakshi in his The Constitution of India (2005).

According to Bakshi, law can regulate—but not take away—the right to administer a religious endowment. The property of a religious endowment can be acquired by the state as well, but 'the core of the religious institution should not be interfered with'.

The Allahabad High Court, which has taken upon itself to divide the disputed site among litigants representing both Muslim and Hindu communities, would appear to have ignored the principle that right of religious institutions cannot be interfered with.

The honourble judges seem to ignore that in our country, the distinction between matters of faith and completely irrational superstitions just does not exist. Myths and epic imaginations such as Thulsidas' Ramcharitmanas and Valmiki's Ramayana are not considered as just popular history mixed with fiction—they are converted into religious faith and superstition by the priestly classes for their own benefits.

Politicians along with priests have become protagonists of religious faith. The politics of faith was seen in its naked form when a mob collected by the Sangh Parivar and led by Bharatiya Janata Party leaders such as LK Advani, Murli Manohar Joshi et al destroyed the mosque in Ayodhya on the plea that Ram temple was destroyed to build the mosque.

The judgment has legitimised vandalism in Ayodhya because this is the language of Mr Advani who maintained that 'matters of faith cannot be decided by the law courts'. If faith and superstition are the basis of jurisprudence, it will be extremely difficult to prevent a segment of society claiming rights over places of worship. Instead of the rule of law, the country will be practicising the law of the jungle in the guise of faith of the believers.

In a country of million deities and little religious traditions, individual groups have been given a handle and a licence to take the law in their hand and occupy any religious place of worship and claim that it is a place of birth of their deity—and courts will be duty-bound to put a stamp of approval to such anarchy. The Allahabad High Court has pronounced a 'dangerous' judgment where a 'deity' has pre-eminent claim over law. Events of December 21/23 night of 1949 when idols of Ram were fraudulently put in the mosque would be repeated by politically-led groups and courts will justify it as a matter of faith.

The Supreme Court should immediately take note of a judgement that is based on extremely 'dangerous' principles, otherwise a plural, democratic and culturally-diverse society will be involved in politically-created religious wars, and this fire will become unextinguishable. Politics has superseded history and faith has supplanted the rule of law, and in this lies the real message of the Allahabad High Court.

—7 October, 2010, The Economic Times

Bihar on Trial

Elections in Bihar, whether for the Lok Sabha or the state assembly, are always a kind of trial for the contesting parties, who wish to win the polls at any cost without caring for any norms of legality. The Election Commission and the state election machinery are on tenterhooks because management of elections in the state is no mean task. Money power and muscle power reign supreme.

This is the context which explains that the forthcoming polls have been staggered into six phases for the maintenance of at least a semblance of law and order during elections for which security forces have to be deployed and redeployed from one place to the other. The state assembly consists of 243 seats and elected representatives have to reflect the social reality of 38 districts of Bihar. In a state defined by a fragmented hierarchy dominated by castes like Bhumihars, Rajputs, Thakurs and Brahmins, the middle social space is occupied by intermediate castes and the surplus generating peasantry followed by extremely backward castes (EBCs) and a good 16 per cent of minorities represented by Muslims and others who have been deprived of the fruits of development and are victims of recurrent floods and drought.

Bihar is a caste-based, fragmented society that has to be mobilised by political parties and party alliances for the winning of an election. The major contestants for the ensuing polls are the JD(U)- BJP alliance, the Congress, the Rashtriya Janata Dal and LOk Janshakti Party alliance and fragments like Janata Dal (Secular), Bahujan Samaj Party et al Not to be left behind are powerful musclemen like Pappu Yadav, Anand Mohan (currently in prison) and Taslimuddin among others. Here it deserves to be pointed out that the phenomenon of criminalisation of politics from the mid-70s began with Bihar and Uttar Pradesh. Not only do important leaders own private armies and musclemen; castes like Bhumihars, Yadavs and Kurmis are a solid caste bloc and these castes vote for their caste leaders only.

The analytical question which draws attention is whether the level of political consciousness in Bihar is equated only with their caste and subcaste identity or the people are attracted towards a performing, development oriented state government. Will the Nitish Kumar agenda and claim of launching Bihar on the journey of development bring political dividends during the elections? Will the state assembly election be a referendum on the developmental agenda of Nitish Kumar or the voters would prefer to have only their caste representatives in the in the Assembly? Will the voters reject the formidable caste based politics of Lalu Prasad and opt for the forward looking, progressive and developmental agenda of Nitish?

During a normal election, the performance of the outgoing party-in-power is x-rayed and votes are cast either against its failure or success. Bihar however is not a normal state in these terms and politics and elections in the state have never been normal because during the last sixty years of post Independence India Bihar's electoral verdicts have been determined by caste-based loyalties; even the Congress and but of course Lalu Prasad Yadav have always been dictated by caste interests of the party in power. A little historical narrative about Bihar is required because society is a product of mass movements either of the famous

Kisan Sabhas and kisan leaders or struggles waged during the Quit India movement of 1942. It requires a deeper analysis as to why post-Independence Bihar has lost its way in the middle and it is remembered only for its glorious history of pre Independence phase when progressive peasant struggles were waged by the masses. Why has Bihar politics degenerated to the level of casteism of the worst kind? Lalu Prasad Yadav proclaimed quite repeatedly that his base of M-Y-Muslims and Yadavs-was solid and impregnable and in spite of his cavalier approach towards administration and his notoriety for misgovernance, he could win elections. If this is the content of Bihar politics, Nitish Kumar may end up as a one time chief minister. The common people of Bihar including a large migrant labouring population of Bihar sing praises of Nitish for his road building project and other employment generating developmental schemes. The rich peasants of Punjab always depended on Bihari migrant agricultural landless labourer to come at the time of harvesting and sowing of crops and they meekly accepted the daily wages as decided by their Punjab employers. This is not the situation now and Nitish Kumar's developmental schemes along with the implementation of the Mahatma Gandhi National Rural Emplyment Guarantee Scheme (NREGA), the labour in distress is not migrating from Bihar because jobs have been created in his own state. Not only this; the Punjab employers during the time of harvesting, sowing and ploughing have to pay more wages to them than they were paid earlier because wage levels in Bihar, their home state, have increased. It is also reported that the completely lawless 'jungle raj' of Lalu Prasad has been up to a great extent been replaced by Nitish's message that law will take its own course while dealing with criminals.

It does not mean that Nitish Kumar's government has established a 'glorious raj' in the state; it only means that his performance has been better than the non-performing predecessors. An important feature of Indian politics, including Bihar, is that power for the sake of power has become the only goal of completely non-ideological contestants. Bihar has witnessed that even while distributing tickets of first out of six phases of elections, the BJP, which has always made tall propaganda about itself as a party of ideology and discipline has faced revolt from its own MLAs who have been denied nomination for elections by the party. Sadhu Yadav of the RJD has walked out of his party because walking out of a party if nomination is denied is a norm and not an exception even in the trump-beater of ideology like the BJP. The real contest in Bihar seems to be triangular as Congress is contesting elections on its own steam and it has been claimed that Rahul Gandhi has galvanized the almost sinking party. The two alliances led by RJD and JD(U) will be the real contestants in the elections. If Yadavs are likely to support Lalu and Sharad, Paswan also has a social constituency of his own. Nitish Kumar is focusing attention on the extremely backward class and he has made special provisions for the EBCs. The 16 per cent Muslim vote is not monolith or a vote bank. Congress is likely to get the support of the Muslims, while Muslims have always voted for the winning candidate and party.

Muslim voters will be divided in their support in the triangular electoral competition. The BJP will not get any electoral support from the Muslims and this is the reason why along with the Congress BJP is also claimant for upper caste votes. Caste/community based demographic profile of Bihar will be reflected during elections and in this context powerful criminals will also have their own stakes as they are in jail. Which side the wind is difficult to predict but one fact about Bihar's elections is that the Development plank versus the caste/community preferences will be tested for the first time. Nitish, while he will support from different castes, has put his performance in the centrestage of electoral drama. Will Bihar society respond to govermentalisation project of Nitish or the same old story of 'caste is god and god is caste' will repeat itself?

—9 October, 2010, The Sahara Time

All in the Name of Public Service

A philosopher once said that amassing of unlimited wealth is not the summum bonum of an individual's life. A politician retorted that the life of an individual is meaningless, if he is not engaged in the pursuit of prosperity. The first statement would commonly be described as utopian and idealistic, while the second one would be deemed quintessentially realistic. Indian politicians are practitioners of such a flawed realism. This, perhaps, is the reason why Union Law Minister M. Veerappa Moily observed that electoral contests today are an expensive affair and this has given rise to corruption in public life. What he tried to imply is that politicians, by means fair or foul, must collect funds.

However, the rising costs of electoral politics is nothing but a poor alibi for the phenomenal growth in the personal wealth of politicians. They adopt every strategy to win an election because a victory can open up unlimited opportunities to maximise their personal resources. Why else has the Election Commission of India appointed expenditure observers for the six-phase elections to the Bihar State Legislature? Why has the Commission decided to appoint an observer for every Bihar State Assembly constituency and one micro-observer, preferably from the Income Tax Department? Why would surprise checks be conducted onboard helicopters used by candidates if these are not used to ferry cash from undisclosed sources? Why has every effort to impose curbs on poll-related expenses been an utter failure? Those who framed laws for the cleansing of the electoral process have been the first to violate them.

Elected representatives of the people are continuously engaged in accumulation of personal wealth by exercising their immense power of patronage. Some Members of Parliament being caught on camera accepting cash to ask questions in the Lok Sabha is not too distant a memory. And, such practices are prevalent in State Assemblies as well. It is common knowledge that some MPs and MLAs protect and promote businessmen and they return the favour in cash or in kind.

In fact, the lawmakers do not hesitate to auction themselves to the highest bidder, abandoning their own party on whose ticket they have been elected. To arrest this phenomenon, the Anti-Defection Law was added to the 10th Schedule of the Indian Constitution in 1985, but our lawmakers refuse to be reined in by concerns of constitutionality where moneymaking is involved. Some MPs even opposed the need for enacting a law to check the practice of 'floor crossing' on the plea that it would crush the right to dissent and give unlimited power to party bosses.

The phenomenon of politics for personal profit is not confined only to individual MPs and MLAs, but has spread its tentacles over political parties which have begun operating on the principle of promoting dynasties. Mrs Indira Gandhi was the founder of this system and she could exercise unlimited control over the tallest of her party leaders because she was the sole repository of huge funds collected by the Congress-in-Government. Significantly, this model of a single dynasty controlling the party could work only if the leader had the sole power to distribute funds to her loyal MPs and MLAs. Many even argue that the Congressmen are not known for their virtues of loyalty and ideological commitment.

Strangely, this system has inspired every leader of regional political formations. Mr M Karunanidhi of the DMK, Mr Sharad Pawar of the Nationalist Congress Party, Mr Lalu Prasad Yadav of Rashtriya Janata Dal, Mr Mulayam Singh Yadav of the Samajwadi Party, Mr Farooq Abdullah and Mr Mufti Mohammad Sayeed, respectively, of the National Conference and People's Democratic Party are little Napoleons of their regional empires. Is democracy safe in the hands of this oligarchy? Even the election of party presidents is a farce as the winner is decided beforehand. There is little chance of a free and fair election under the leadership of those who conduct fake polls within their own parties. In the absence of inner-party democracy, politicians prosper under the benign patronage of a dynasty and loyalty to him provides them complete immunity.

—22 October, 2010, The Pioneer

Trouble Piles up for Embattled Congress

Congress president Sonia Gandhi is going through one of the worst phases of her career as the leader of the party with the Congress suffering an election debacle in Bihar, faced with a leadership crisis in Andhra Pradesh and mired in corruption controversy in Maharashtra. Ms Gandhi has performed an excellent job of reviving the Congress, which was sliding downwards in the 1990s, during the first decade of the 21st century. The Congress has recognised her contribution in rebuilding a decaying party by electing her as the party president for the fourth term this year. The party had to accept Ms Gandhi's leadership because she is the only all-India leader of the party. And in true legacy of Congress's dynasty politics, only she could bring all factions together. All other leaders like Mr Pranab Mukherjee, Mr P Chidambaram, or Mr SM Krishna have limited political influence, which is co-terminus with the States they belong to.

However, Ms Gandhi must be worried because not only has she failed to manage the party organisation effectively at the State levels, but under her stewardship the party has failed to show any electoral successes in major North Indian States. The electoral verdict of Bihar proves that neither Ms Gandhi, nor Mr Rahul Gandhi could cut much ice, in spite of their active campaigning. Instead of increasing its strength, the Congress party lost five out of nine seats it had won in the elections of October 2005, obtaining only four Assembly seats in a House of 243. The party's strategy of contesting the elections of 2010 on its own came a 'cropper' and its local leaders like Mr Mukul Wasnik and Mr Anil Sharma proved complete failure to mobilise the local Congress party workers. Ms Gandhi admitted in a Press conference on November 24 that the party would have to begin from scratch in Bihar as she realised that a non-existing party cannot compete during the elections.

If it is difficult for Ms Gandhi to swallow the bitter pill of a humiliating defeat in Bihar, it is all the more problematic to manage a faction-ridden party in the States. The Congress leadership was absolutely clueless on how to deal with YS Rajasekhara Reddy's son Mr Jaganmohan Reddy, who has been consistently taking pot shots at the party's central leadership and made the life of Mr K. Rosaiah, who the High Command nominated as Chief Minister after the death of YSR Reddy, hell. The 14 month tenure of Mr K. Rosaiah, a nominee of Ms Gandhi, became a bed of thorns because Mr Jaganmohan Reddy had refused to accept him as a replacement of his late father.

The worst crisis for an undisputed leader of the party arises when its own writ does not run within the party. She hesitated to discipline the rebel leader, although he launched a scathing attack against the central leadership through his TV channel Sakshi. The TV held Ms Gandhi responsible for the party's "degeneration" and dubbed the Prime Minister as "rubber stamp", but Ms Gandhi kept quiet. The political developments within the Andhra Congress have completely exposed Ms Gandhi's poor leadership as she has completely failed to provide any guidance to Andhra Congress leaders on how to tackle the agitation on the demand for a separate Telangana State.

The greatest challenge to Ms Gandhi's leadership has been posed by the BJP because she has not been able to evolve any political strategy to displace BJP State Governments in North India like Madhya Pradesh, Gujarat and Chhattisgarh, where the BJP got re-elected. The State-level Congress leaders have neither been able to corner the Chief Ministers of these States nor mobilise the party organisation.

Ms Gandhi seems to be a poor learner about the inner dynamics of party system because she has failed to understand that her style of 'centralisation' and nominations of PCC presidents and Chief Ministers simply doesn't work. The Congress party hardly has an organisation in Bihar and her decision to send central leaders to Bihar to provide stewardship to the party proved a non-starter. The Gujarat Congress does not have a leader to match the stature of Mr Narendra Modi. It has been repeatedly proved that the absence of strong local leader at the State levels has brought defeats to the party. The new Maharashtra Chief Minister or the replacement for Mr Rosaiah have been nominated by Ms Gandhi. Only she has forgotten that Mr Rosaiah and Mr Ashok Chavan were also nominated by her. This strategy has failed to click because it has not led to the revitalisation of the Congress organisation at the grassroots level in the States. The local Congress workers need a leader with enough mass base who will be acceptable to the voters of the State. Ms Gandhi must democratise the Congress and let leaders be elected by local Congress workers. If she does not allow local leaders to emerge in the States, she will fail to rejuvenate the party and win elections. Unlike Mrs Indira Gandhi, she has failed to learn how to establish the political chemistry between a woman leader and her voters.

—20 November, 2010, The Pioneer

Institutionalisation of Corruption

In a democracy, political leaders lose their credibility, even legitimacy, if voters develop a perception that their elected representatives are abusing and misusing power for self-enrichment and engage in crass favouritism. Verily, even democracy will gain a bad name in the process. People were stunned when Ratan Tata said recently that a minister of aviation had asked him for a bribe for a routine permission to expand Tata's project of airlines in collaboration with a Singapore company.

Then came the 2G scam and the mindboggling amount of money involved in it. Clearly, the erstwhile minister of telecommunication, A Raja, had flouted every rule, regulation and procedure by distributing telecom licences to companies and individuals on the first-come-first-served basis, instead of auctioning them in the open market through fair bidding.

Ironically, the decision to appoint Raja as telecommunications minister was taken by DMK supremo M Karunanidhi, not the Prime Minister. Hence, every leader of every party in a coalition government is a party to the malfunctioning and malgovernance at the Centre. Corruption in one party-led government is appropriated by a single source of power but in a coalition system, every partner claims a share in the spoils of office. Is it fatalistically determined that ccrruption in public life will increase in the age of coalition governments?

Similarly, Karnataka chief minister BS Yeddyurappa has been playing a cat-and mouse game after it has been established that he misused his authority for land-grabbing. Yet, the BJP can't remove him from office because of votebank considerations. Post-Nehru governments in India have not been able to punish the guilty ministers or chief ministers because resignation is not a punishment enough to prevent the gross abuse of power. The acts of corruption by public functionaries take place quite regularly because there is no effective deterrence to nail the culprits. Raja or Ashok Chavan or even Yeddyurappa will continue to pollute public life because even after their exit, they enjoy the protective umbrella and patronage of their respective parties and leaders.

Veerappa Moily has publicly stated that the mounting

electioneering expenditures are responsible for the rising level of corruption. LK Advani, on the other hand, has consistently pleaded for the public funding of elections to cleanse the body politic of corruption. What is conveniently forgotten in the debate is the point that politicians have themselves converted the electoral process into an ugly competition of money power.

Further, it has been suggested that the quantum of corruption has increased by leaps and bounds because every partner in a coalition government operates as an 'empire within an empire' and every political group separately accumulates funds by exercising power. Is it any wonder then that that every partner in a coalition government stakes claims to the ministries where more money can be milked through kickbacks?

Every chief election commissioner has attracted public attention to the pernicious role that 'money power' plays during elections. However, every party has seen to it that autonomous institutions like Lok Pal and Lok Ayukta that could expose and curb corruption in public life have been reduced to the status of paper tigers.

Every major political party, national or regional, is dominated and controlled by a family or extra-constitutional authority like the RSS. The supreme or real controllers of a party machine also need immense financial resources to distribute favours to their political favourites in these private political shops. The loyal party men know it quite well that their leaders would take care of their financial needs during their political career.

As a consequence of this, corruption spreads like a tornado in public life, smashing the normal procedure-based system of governance in democracy. India cannot remain an exception to this rule. The credibility of the CBI or the Central Vigilance Commission as autonomous watchdogs has been eroded because politicians cannot allow these agencies to bring out the skeletons in their cupboards. In fact, there are more incentives in our system to shield corruption: why should a civil servant oblige a minister without getting a share of public funds for his own private family purposes?

Corruption in pubic life can be uprooted only if the guilty are punished and the fear of the rule of law acts as a deterrent among politicians and bureaucrats. For this to happen, we need speedy trial and justice dispensed by agencies autonomous in letter and spirit—agencies that operate without any fear or favour of the politicians. During his time as the PM, Jawaharlal

Nehru had showed us the way by removing every minister who had been tainted with the charge of corruption.

We have to follow this route of inflicting heavy punishments on public functionaries involved in loot and plunder and confiscate their property and freeze their bank accounts.

—27 November, 2010, The Economic Times

Future Bleak for Both National Parties

The two former poles of national politics are now struggling to retain their old identities. Without State party support both face existential threats. For the BJP, the problem is more acute because it has isolated the Muslim voters

Nitish Kumar's victory in the Bihar elections of November 2010 has once again brought into sharp focus the future prospects of the National Democratic Alliance (NDA) at the centre for the Lok Sabha elections of 2014. The euphoria generated by the electoral victories of Janata Dal (United) and BJP is based not on the success of the NDA but also because by winning 206 out 243 seats in the State Assembly, the Alliance has completely decimated and annihilated the Opposition parties like Lalu Prasad's Rashtriya Janata Dal, Ram Vilas Paswan's Lok Jan Shakti Party, the Communists and especially the Congress which has been completely routed by winning just 4 seats out of 243 in the Bihar Assembly.

The NDA has encouraged erstwhile partners of the Atal Bihari Vajpayee-led government from 1998 to 2004 to think that a wave is blowing against the Congress and its allies and that the voters' choice is shifting towards an alternative political coalition to the present Congress-led UPA government at the Centre. The Election Commission has recognised six national parties and 50 State parties. The Congress and the BJP are the two principal poles of national politics and other regional parties are always prepared to join the coalition government in which either the Congress or the BJP is able to win sizable seats at an all-India level. The future dreams of the revival of NDA as an alternative centre of power are based on the ground reality prevailing in the different States of India.

The natural political allies of the anti-Congress coalition are Akali Dal of Punjab, Om Prakash Chauthala of Lok Dal of Haryana, Mayawati of the Bahujan Samaj Party of Uttar Pradesh, Shiv Sena of Maharashtra, Chandrababu Naidu of Telugu Desam party of Andhra Pradesh, the Communist parties of Kerala and West Bengal, AASU and AGP of Assam, and Navin Patnaik of Biju Janata Dal of Orissa. All these well-established regional political formations are competing against the Congress in their State and these competitors are committed to anti-Congressim at the

Centre. These regional parties cannot join any coalition led by the Congress. Not only this. These anti-Congress State level parties are natural allies of anti-Congress BJP, which has a government of its own in the States of Himachal Pradesh, Madhya Pradesh, Chhattisgarh, Uttarkhand, Gujarat and Karnataka and also an alliance partner in governments of Punjab, Jharkhand, and Bihar. BJP and these competitors against the Congress in their own States occupy a sizable political space and are always present in the Lok Sabha. Navin Patanik of the BJD had an alliance with the BJP which collapsed but he is a pillar of anti-Congressim in Orissa.

The doubtful and dubious leaders in the game of coalition making at the centre are Ajit Singh of Rahstriya Janata Dal of Uttar Pradesh, Shibu Soren of Jharkhand Mukti Morcha, Ram Vilas Paswan of Lok Janatantrik Party of Bihar, Mamata Banejree of Trinamool Congress, and M Karunanidhi and Km Jayalalithaa of the DMK and AIADMK of Tamil Nadu because everyone of them is ready to ally with anyone to capture power at the Centre.

The greatest limitation of BJP in forging a future coalition government at the Centre lies in the crisis it is facing with its own leaders. The BJP-led State government of Karnataka is crisis-ridden because its own Chief Minister is alleged to be the 'land grabber' and Karnataka Lok Ayukta is investigating the land deals concluded by the BJP government.

The Janata Dal chief, Sharad Yadav, who is also a convener of the NDA, is quite cautious about his party's close association with the BJP and at the same time maintains a respectable distance from its leadership. If anti-Congress forces of Uttar Pradesh and Bihar come together for a future coalition, a BJP Prime Minister may not be acceptable to the players in those states' caste conundrums. Besides, a Mamata Banerjee who has to deal with a 26 per cent Muslim vote base and a Navin Patanik would balk at the suggestion.

The BJP cannot replicate its model of 1998 to 2004 when it led the NDA coalition government because many of its future allies who are committed to 'anti-Congress' politics are hesitant to accepting its leadership. LK Advani attacked genuine secularists as 'pseudo' because of the Muslim factor in the calculations of politics. But the reality is that the majority of regional parties are 'pseudo secularist' because they want to co-habit with the BJP without alienating the Muslim political constituency. Even these 'pseudo-secular' and anti-Congress political formations are allergic to the idea of open and public commitment with a BJP leadership. These pseudo-secular anti-Congress regionalists want to eat the cake and also keep it.

The future for both BJP and the Congress, the two poles of national politics, is not quite bright because BJP is facing crisis of leadership and the Congress is facing serious political and electoral challenges in the major States.

—2 December, 2010, The Pioneer

Meaning of the Verdict

The JD(U)-BJP alliance succeeded in trouncing RJD, LJP and also the Congress in the elections by capturing three-fourths of the Assembly seats—an incredible win, never witnessed since the 1970s elections. The other remarkable feature of the elections was that women and the poorest of the poor decided to exercise their right to vote without any fear of musclemen, criminals and gun-wielding goons who would terrorise voters and indulge in booth capturing. Bihar is known to be synonymous with 'criminalisation of politics' as elections in the state were always held under the sword of Damocles of the goons and musclemen. Nitish Kumar, while addressing a press conference, also highlighted this fact by stating that in earlier elections, either the candidates or the supporters had been brutally injured by musclemen. It is a grand success of democracy that in a state like Bihar, the Assembly elections were violence-free.

The significance of "violence-free elections" lies in the fact that the preceding regime of Lalu Prasad was identified with "Goonda Raj" and complete lawlessness prevailed in Bihar during the RJD rule. Nitish had contested both the 2005 elections of February and October-November against Lalu's lawless regime where ordinary citizens lived in fear. The people of Bihar were ready to accept an alternative to Lalu's lawless regime because security of life and property was always the first priority of a peace-loving citizen. Nitish Kumar, as chief minister, kept his promise of providing a regime based on law and order and he could boldly claim that the streets of Patna were safe from hooligans, kidnappers and murderers.

Developmental activities can never take place in an unsafe atmosphere. And by enforcing law and order, Nitish's government managed to send a message to investors, businessmen and traders that Bihar was safe for economic activities.

Nitish's record of governance, both in the field of maintaining law and order in the state and ensuring basic amenities, and services like building of roads *et al* have paid rich dividends in the elections. The art of politics lies in the message the voters receive from their leaders and Nitish successfully conveyed the message that he is for economic development of Bihar. The voters were appreciative of Nitish's effort to bring Bihar back to the path of development because Bihari pride was hurt when Bihar was ridiculed for poverty, ignorance, illiteracy and forced and distress migration for employment to inhospitable places like Mumbai or Delhi. The Biharification of Delhi-based universities and colleges happened because Bihar's educational system had collapsed and the youth of Bihar were compelled to leave the state for education. It is a pity that the fertile state of Bihar could not retain its own workforce, which migrated to unknown places for attaining just subsistence levels. So, this hurt psyche of an ordinary Bihari was partly restored by developmental activities of Nitish Kumar and by creating some new job opportunities during the last five years. It is a well-known fact that the image of a leader is either a liability or an asset. While Lalu became a liability, Nitish Kumar's image as a "doer, a developer, an administrator" caught the imagination of the voters. Nitish's image has brought great electoral dividends for the JD(U) and BJP combine.

What about the performance of the Congress? It had been claimed that there is a lot of political space which lies vacant between Lalu and Nitish and thus it will provide an opportunity to the Congress to emerge as a sole "balancer". It did not happen as Congress' strategy of occupying the alternative space in Bihar politics collapsed and the myth surrounding Rahul Gandhi's youth leadership is lying in shambles. Nitish evolved an electoral strategy by fragmenting Lalu and Paswan's social constituency and created schisms in the backward castes by patronising the Extremely Backward Classes (EBC) and Paswan's Dalit base by separating Mahadalits from the dominant Paswan Dalits. It is simplistic to maintain that caste has not played its central role in Bihar election, but on the contrary, castes have been further fragmented by Nitish and JD(U).

Bihar minus caste is a society without any other reference point of identity of its own. Hence, caste identities have played their role even during the elections and the only difference this time is—"caste plus development"— which has played a decisive role in the elections.

The election of Nitish Kumar has raised people's hopes and expectations and in his press conference, he maintained that "he does not have the Alladin's lamp" but he would make sincere efforts to develop Bihar. Indira Gandhi had also raised high hopes after getting two-third majority in the Lok Sabha election of 1971 and her slogan of "Garibi Hatao" had electrified the voters. This high hope is a two-edged weapon because....

when hopes are not satisfied, the anger of voters is directed against the leader. This is precisely what happened with Indira Gandhi. Nitish may fall in the same trap if he does not fulfill the hopes and expectations of the voters. Bihar has followed "the agenda of development" which is a good bet for winners. Beware Nitish! And fear your popularity

—4 December, 2010, Rashtriya Saraha Weekly

Politics Beyond Stalled Parliament

As the Congress-led UPA government and the BJP-led Opposition could not agree on an appropriate mechanism of inquiry to go into the procedures followed by former telecommunication minister A Raja on 2G spectrum allocation, the whole winter session of Parliament got disrupted.

As the Opposition insisted on forming a joint parliamentary committee (JPC) to probe 2G scam, the session ended without transacting any business at all. The Opposition has not only announced a mass agitation, it has also warned that if a JPC is not formed, the Budget session will also meet the same fate.

Why are the government and the Opposition not trying to find a middle way to end the parliamentary deadlock? Why is it that neither the government nor the Opposition is interested in finding a middle path on the 2G scam? The Congress has alleged that the BJP is demanding a JPC for purely political reasons and it is not at all interested in fighting against corruption in public life because its own leaders have been corrupt while in power.

Congress president Sonia Gandhi has repeatedly stated the BJP has not forgotten its electoral defeats in 2004 and 2009, and is now trying to build a broader anti-Congress coalition based on the 2G scam.

This is the crux of the issue. The BJP is a committed anti-Congress politico-cultural and socio-religious formation and it is trying to corner the Congress in states and regions where real electoral battles are won and lost. The BJP has not only expanded both spatially and ideologically, but also feels quite confident that it can successfully form an anti-Congress front with the full support of regional, sub-regional and casteist parties and repeat its performance of 1998 and 1999. As it stands now, the Congress looks quite vulnerable in every large state of India, including in its present strongholds of Maharashtra and Andhra Pradesh.

The political map of India is in a fragmented position. Hence, both the Congress and the BJP are engaged in attracting multiple political groups around its own bloc of power. The communists are committed anti-Congress and anti-BJP political groupings, but they lack the capacity to lead a non-BJP, non-Congress third front. Every attempt of the leftist parties to form a third front that is equidistant from the Congress and the BJP has ended in utter fiasco and they are not likely to get any benefit by boycotting Parliament on the demand for a JPC.

So, this tripolar front politics is, in reality, reduced to a bipolar contest between the Congress and the BJP. At the national level, most other parties will just yield their loyalty to the party that is capable of forming a government at the Centre.

Therefore, the real political game in sorting out the issue of immobilised Parliament will be played by the Congress and the BJP. The BJP's target is to create rift within the UPA allies and bring around waverers like the Trinamool Congress and a few others to force the government to concede the Opposition demand for JPC so that it can target the Prime Minister for his acts of omission and commission while dealing with the misdoings of his erstwhile cabinet colleague A Raja.

On the other hand, the Congress strategy to break the parliamentary deadlock is to convince public opinion and some opposition parties that the existing institutions like the Central Bureau of Investigation, enforcement directorate, income tax department, Public Accounts Committee of Parliament and the Comptroller and Auditor General are at work on the case.

The party claims that these agencies are competent to unearth the wrongdoings, if any, of the ministry of telecommunication, lobbyist Niira Radia, and bureaucrats like former TRAI chief Pradeep Baijal and many others who joined Radia's multiple public relations firms. The party contends that the Manmohan Singh government has nothing to hide on 2G spectrum allocation and all investigations are open to public scrutiny because the Supreme Court has decided to oversee all public agencies engaged in probing the scam. What else can be done by the government in a case like this?

The impact of this reasoning has already been felt and the Janata Dal (Secular) and the Biju Janata Dal have decided to dissociate themselves from the protests organised by the BJP-led NDA allies. More parties are likely to follow the suit and the Budget session may not see the repeat performance of the deadlocked winter session.

The involvement of Supreme Court in monitoring the 2G scam probe will be welcomed by the public at large. It is quite probable that the parliamentary deadlock will come to an end when the Budget session begins because small groups would leave the leading players but the two Front Bloc politics will remain on the political landscape of India. The BJP is determined to regain power at the Centre and it has no dearth of regional allies and the Congress has to fight against the BJP's revival. Politics of mobilisation has begun, and Parliament's normalcy will return.

—25 December, 2010, The Economic Times

Reaping the Fruits of Economic Growth

That the Heads of Government of all five permanent members of the UN Security Council, namely the US, the UK, China, France and Russia, visited India this year serves to underscore India's increased importance in the international arena. While British, French, American and Russian leaders hailed India as their strategic partner, Chinese premier Wen Jiabao's policy statements made during the visit deserve to be carefully analysed because India's expectations from China are fundamentally different from its expectations from other countries. The two neighbours have quite a few knotty issues to resolve.

In a way, the Indian foreign policy-makers have been partially successful because they could make some leaders come up with unambiguous statements condemning Pakistan-exported terrorism. While British Prime Minister David Cameron and French President Nicolas Sarkozy have unequivocally asked Pakistan to stop allowing Islamist radicals use its territory for sinister activities against India, US President Barack Obama made a 'cautious' comment, keeping in view Pakistan's importance as an ally in fighting the Taliban and the Al Qaeda in Afghanistan and in dealing with Arab nations. Although Mr Obama pontificated that India should start engaging with Pakistan starting with 'less contentious issues and then go to controversial ones' because India has 'the biggest stake in ensuring a secure, stable Pakistan', he should have remembered what his predecessor Mr George Bush wrote in his book *Decision Days:* "Almost every conversation we had, Gen Musharraf accused India of wrong doing". India-Pakistan relations hinge a lot on the Pakistan Army, which is known to harbour malicious intent of destabilising India while accusing the Indian Army of creating unrest in the restive province of Balochistan.

However, the Chinese story is more complicated. As Chinese Ambassador to India Zhang Yan has aptly stated before Mr Wen Jiabao's visit: "China-India relations are very fragile and very easy to be damaged and very difficult to repair". Although Foreign Secretary Nirupama Rao has stated that India has expressed its concerns about terrorism "emanating from Pakistani soil", Mr Jiabao maintained a studied silence on the issue.

The most important result of Mr Jiabao's visit has been the 'operationalisation of the hotline' between the two countries and an agreement that Foreign Ministers of both countries will meet every year. All other 'core concerns' of India were left for further negotiations. However, Mr Jiabao on the Pakistan-leg of his visit observed that terrorism "cannot be linked with any particular country or religion" making evident its closeness to India's arch-rival Pakistan. Given the strategic aspect of the China-Pakistan relationship and all the attendant complexities, the essence of India-China relationship lies in competition, collaboration and continuous engagement between the two neighbouring countries.

The Foreign Policy Resolution passed at the AICC session of the Congress on December 20, 2010 acknowledged that India's engagement with the US has been 'a major transformation'. The Congress has endorsed the Government's 'pro-America' foreign policy and welcomed 'intensification of ties with China'.

However, India cannot expect an all-out support either from America or from China on the very contentious issue of terrorism originating from Pakistan. India will have to fight its own battle. How can Mr Obama's India visit change US-Pakistan strategic alliance on war in Afghanistan? How can Mr Jiabao's India visit bring any change in the close bilateral relationship between China and Pakistan? Another factor that conditions China's responses to India is India's perceived 'tilt' towards the US because the Chinese always have been wary of India-America close collaborations.

The growing closeness between India and other countries is just a reflection of the new reality—that India's economy is growing at tremendous speed. For instance, Mr Jiabao came to India with more than 300 business dignitaries. Hence, India's foreign policy is getting new economic dimensions and more should not be read into the Joint Communiqué of the visiting dignitaries. The visiting Heads of Government have made agreements with India on bilateral trade and sale of defence equipment, although these are being heralded as great foreign policy achievement with five permanent members of the UN Security Council.

What India should look for is strategic relations which are meaningful for India's security. Only Russian President Dmitry Medvedev, of all the five leaders, made a forthright statement on December 23: "When I visited India four days after the Mumbai attacks I told them (the Government) ...we are ready to provide weapons, modern technology and know-how".

He openly reiterated Russia's stand of supporting India "if they ever take a hard decision against a friendly neighbouring country". Sadly, the UPA Government has always taken Russia's support for granted and made an extra effort to win American friendship, knowing fully well that the US has 'special bonds' with Pakistan. The Government of the day has forgotten that the foreign policy of 'equi-distance' and equal friendship has always paid rich dividends and currying special favours from America has never borne the fruits. Terrorism from across the border is India's problem and it has to solve the issue with Pakistan on its own. The foreign Governments will only extend lip-service. The top priority of India's foreign policy should be focussed on strengthening relations with neighbouring countries so that China doesn't take advantage of the vacuum created.

—30 December, 2010, The Pioneer

Convergence of Ideas Needed to Fight Maoists

Since May 2009 Minister for Home Affairs P Chidambaram has been unequivocally stating that Maoism is the greatest internal security threat to the country. In a recent statement, he has observed, "The conflict with Maoist groups escalated and remained the biggest headache for security forces in the year gone by". He has substantiated his observation with facts: A total of 713 civilians were killed by Maoist groups in 2010, as compared to 591 in 2009. While Maoists had only 171 casualties, security forces lost 285 personnel in 2^10, a tad less than 317 killed in 2009. It clearly shows that Maoist groups enjoyed an upper hand while security forces struggled to contain violence. Hence, the question is how the Union Government and State Governments witnessing Maoist insurgency should respond to the challenge. Do the political and bureaucratic executives of the Union and State Governments have any consensus on responses to the threat posed by Maoists?

While addressing the Central Reserve Police Forces or Indian Police officials, Prime Minister Manmohan Singh, Minister for Finance Pranab Mukherjee and Mr Chidambaram have often asked them to deal with Maoist extremism 'firmly and resolutely'. If this is the strategy of the Union Government, then it has to take along the State Governments with it because fighting against Maoist insurgency is a joint responsibility of the Union Government and the States. However, Mr Chidambaram has created a rift between the Union Government and the West Bengal Government by shooting a letter to Chief Minister Buddhadeb Bhattacharjee in December last year, criticising the 'alarming law and order situation' in the State. He accused the armed cadres of CPI(M), 'Harmad Vahini', of spreading violence, especially against political opponents. Mr Bhattacharjee repudiated the charge calling Mr Chidambaram's assessment of the situation as "surprising" and "far from impartial". It is common knowledge that the West Bengal Government is fighting against Maoists with great determination.

However, it has accused Congress's alliance partner Trinamool Congress of aligning with Maoist groups to gain political mileage before the forthcoming Assembly election. But the Union Government has looked the other way. How can any State Government fight against Maoists without undiluted support from the Union Government?

The UPA2 Government is not at odds only with the West Bengal Government when it comes to dealing with Maoism. Jharkhand Mukti Morcha leader Shibu Soren and Chief Minister of Bihar Nitish Kumar also are not in line with the Union Government's strategy. Mr Nitish Kumar has maintained that Maoism has social roots and it cannot be treated solely as a 'law and order' problem. On the other hand, the JMM has allegedly taken the support of Maoist activists during the Jharkhand State Assembly election as a *quid pro quo* arrangement because Maoists wanted protection from paramilitary forces. The only upshot is that Prime Minister Manmohan Singh and his Cabinet colleagues seem to have finally realised that Maoism is not just a 'law and order' issue but has its roots in the society. They have acknowledged that gun-wielding Maoists have been successful in establishing bases in nine States of India because gut-wrenching poverty in tribal areas has created serious discontent among locals. The Prime Minister, while addressing the IPS probations on December 25, 2010, said, "You must have the sensitivity to recognise the social and economic roots of disaffection among tribal societies where Maoism has become a major force to reckon with." Mr Mukherjee on December 29 has stated that armed operations against Maoists "must be dovetailed with development" as people have been "denied their legitimate demands" and "deprived of their rights".

Accordingly, the UPA2 Government has sanctioned ₹ 13,000 crore for special development of 60 Maoist-affected districts in Odisha, Jharkhand, Chhattisgarh, Madhya Pradesh, Bihar, West Bengal and Uttar Pradesh. This is a follow-up of the Planning Commission's Integrated Action Plan for Maoist-hit districts. The emphasis of this special development programme will be on health, education, drinking water and roads. The criteria for the identification of special schemes for these 60 districts are: It should have 25 per cent of tribal population. At least 50 per cent of the local population should be living 'below the poverty line'. And security-related considerations should be kept in mind while identifying the nature of services needed for these districts.

Besides, both the Union Government and State Governments have launched other special schemes and earmarked special funds for backward regions.

Taking into account leakages of welfare funds during the implementation process, the Union Government has decided to form an Implementation Committee consisting of District Collector, Superintendent of Police and Forest Development Officer. That the committee will be held solely responsible for the implementation of such programmes is a welcome move but local tribal people must be involved in the implementation of programmes meant for their welfare.

Having said that, the real bottlenecks in policy planning have been the inconsistency in the Union Government's approach to Maoist insurgency and the clash of perspectives between the Union Government and the States.

— 17 January, 2011, The Pioneer

Corruption Impacts Governance

It is rare that public leaders with impeccable credentials address 'An open letter to our leaders', pointing to the 'governance deficit' in the country owing to public institutions impaired by the 'growing cancer of corruption in the body-politic'.

Alluding to a slew of corruption scandals that came into public view in the past one year, Ashok Ganguly, the spokesman of the group of eminent persons, observed on January 17: 'We have felt that we should not be silent on the issue. A large section of the Indian population is deeply perturbed by the series of events that unfolded in the recent past." The sum and substance of this is that political parties must wake up to this reality or else it will be too late to stem the rot in governance.

It is ironical that the warning has been issued by industry and business leaders because the general perception is that it's the businessmen who corrupt politics. It's also amusing to see political parties accusing each other of indulging in corruption in public life even though it's common knowledge that none of them is clean.

Western democracies have well-laid laws for regulating political parties. India, too, has established an autonomous Election Commission for the conduct and supervision of elections and for enforcing the 'code of conduct' for parties during polls. India also has the Representation of People Act, in which norms for the conduct of people's elected 'representatives' are laid down. It is legally binding on every party to hold regular organisational elections for its office-bearers as laid down by the written constitution of each party. It is mandatory for every contestant in state assembly or Lok Sabha elections to submit a full statement of assets to the Election Commission. The Right to Information Act 2005 has given freedom to every citizen to ask any elected representative to provide facts about his 'real assets' to the public.

Of course, political parties in every competitive democracy require funds to contest polls and to maintain their organisation. Hence, it is mandatory for every political party to 'maintain a record of the names and addresses of people who voluntarily make donations exceeding 20,000' and the income tax (IT) department provides tax exemptions to parties on the basis of their 'account books'. If developed democratic societies have been able to regulate the conduct of political parties according to their laws, Indians should also have succeeded in regulating parties on the basis of a comprehensive legal framework regulating parties, their finances and conduct during the elections. Unfortunately, that is not the case.

The Election Commission has recognised six parties as 'national' and more than 50 as 'state parties' and mandated that every recognised party has to hold regular inner-party elections. However, the root cause of the corrupt and undemocratic functioning of parties is the basic lack of inner-party democracy. Sonia Gandhi is elected and re-elected as Congress president and only she is 'authorised' with 'full powers' to nominate state party presidents. The BJP gets Nitin Gadkari as its president because he is the nominee of the RSS chief Mohan Bhagwat. Every 'recognised' regional party, too, is run like a private family business under the thumb of Karunanidhis, Mulayam Singhs or Lalu Prasads. The supreme leaders have an iron grip over their parties because all funds for their outfits have to be only deposited with them. Often, no one within the parties knows much about the sources of funds.

The Election Commission has made persistent efforts to clean up the election campaigning finance structure. During the 2010 Bihar assembly election, it sent its expenditure observers, a 'video viewing' team, a media monitoring team and an observer preferably from the IT department. This vigilance initiative revealed some shocking facts. It was found that fraudulent parties are floated to launder money. Actually, checks revealed that office of one such party was in a tea shop, while another spent 2-3 crore on jewellery and shares, and many of these so-called 'political parties' have not participated in elections for the last several years.

The US has a law to regulate lobbyists who influence political decision-makers on behalf of corporate bodies. After the revelations about lobbyist Neera Radia, a demand was made that India should also have such a law for the registration of lobbyists. It has been suggested by the late Ramakrishna Hegde and Dinesh Goswami, in their reports on election reforms, that 'parties should be funded from the public exchequer' for contesting elections as it will help cleanse public life once parties do not depend on private donors. The Election Commission has not found this recommendation feasible, perhaps on the basis of its own experiences with the reality of elections and role of parties.

While all efforts should be made to cleanse the political system, the expectations should be quite modest. India requires more interventions from the leading lights of public life like Sonia Gandhi to highlight the serious crisis of governance that is the logical product of corruption in politics.

—21 January, 2011, The Economic Times

India under UPA is Facing Serious Governance Deficit

It deserves to be clearly stated that India under the Congress-led UPA Government is facing serious governance deficit which is adversely affecting the country. Prime Minister Manmohan Singh has failed to evolve appropriate policies to curb the rising food inflation, which has hit the common man hard. The Ministers have offered phoney excuses to escape their responsibilities. All assurances that the inflation will come down have proved to be wrong. The Congress looks clueless and directionless in dealing with the problem of rising food prices.

Prime Minister Manmohan Singh and UPA chairperson Sonia Gandhi have also failed to counter effectively the allegations of corruption and misrule. The Winter session of Parliament last year could not function properly because the Opposition was not satisfied with the Government's response on the issue of 2G Spectrum sale or swindling of money in the Commonwealth Games. The dust has still not settled. The issue of evasion of income tax and siphoning of black money out of India has complicated matters. The Supreme Court of India has pointed out that depositing national money of India in foreign banks amounts to 'loot of national wealth'. However, Minister for Finance Pranab Mukherjee in his Press conference on January 24 did not come forward with any concrete strategy to bring back the money, which is stashed away in foreign banks.

Why is the UPA Government incapable of responding to challenges facing the country? A few facts may be mentioned to substantiate the argument that the UPA Government has failed because of the 'dual leadership'. Ms Gandhi is not only the president of the Congress party, she is the supreme leader whose writ runs in the Government. Leaders of the party organisation and Congress Ministers in the Government are accountable to her. Ms Gandhi's complete control over party's organisational structure can be extremely helpful to the Congress-led Government if she acts as the eyes and ears of the party and provides feedback to the Government about the grievances of the people.

As president of the Congress, she is expected to act as a link between the party organisation and the Government. But Ms Gandhi, it seems, is not satisfied with such a passive role but wants to lead the party as well as the Government without being a formal office holder. The Prime Minister consults Ms Gandhi on all matters that fall in the domain of governance and for which he is solely responsible under the Constitution of India.

The party president can advise or make suggestions to the Prime Minister, but cannot act as an alternative source of making public policies in parliamentary system. The UPA Government is at loggerheads with Ms Gandhi's 'super Cabinet', the National Advisory Council, on a very important issue—of the modalities of implementation of the much-awaited Food Secuirty Bill.

The experts in the Government are not agreeing to the suggestions of NAC on the criterion of determining the rural and urban populations to be covered by this scheme. The public controversy between the Government and Ms Gandhi on public policy issues has not only sent wrong signals to the country, but has conveyed the message that NAC is a 'super Cabinet' and Ms Gandhi is the source of authority.

The NAC is also engaged in a tug of war with the Union Government on the issue of 'wages' paid under Mahatma Gandhi National Rural Employment Guarantee scheme. Ms Gandhi has suggested to the Union Government that under MNREGA minimum wages should be paid as 'laid down by the laws of the land'. But the Government has expressed its inability to oblige because according to Government calculations, the burden will be too heavy on the public exchequer. Ms Gandhi's suggestions to the Government on Food Secuirty Bill, minimum wages under MNREGA or the proposed amendments in the RTI Act gives the impression that it is not Mr Singh who is leading the Government, but Ms Gandhi is the real centre of power.

Further, Mr Rahul Gandhi's recommendations to the Government have far more weightage than the recommendations of any other Congress leader because he shines in the reflected glory of his mother. It is the prerogative of the Congress to decide whether it wants to make Mr Gandhi a Minister or even a Prime Minister, but he is harming the democratic system by participating in policy matters, which is not his responsibility as an ordinary MP.

Ms Gandhi to her credit has rejuvenated and revived the declining

Congress party and the party leaders accept her undisputed supremacy in the organisation. However, her special status as Congress president must not impact the functioning of Congress-led Governments at the Centre and the States. Congress party should remember that former Prime Minister Jawaharlal Nehru had publicly conveyed to Congress president JB Kripalani that he is not expected to meddle with the affairs of the Government. Jawaharlal Nehru also took on Purushotam Das Tandon, another Congress president, because he was not in tune with the thinking and ideological make-up of the party and it eventually led to Tandon's resignation.

The Prime Minister is the real leader of the country and there can be no 'dual' or 'triple' centres of power in a parliamentary democracy. If Mr Singh is perceived as 'passive' and Ms Gandhi is projected as the 'real source of power' of the Government, then it not only affects governance, it also harms the image of the Congress. That way neither is Ms Gandhi serving the interest of her party nor the interest of the UPA Government, where her party is the major stakeholder. Unless she amends her interfering attitude, the Government will become counter-productive and the Congress will have to pay the price in the next election.

—31 January, 2011, The Pioneer

Judicial Activism can Prove Harmful

A section of the educated and articulate urban middle-class has come to believe, quite erroneously, that the ills of political system can be eradicated by judicial interventions. It deserves to be clearly stated that political process cannot be reformed and its evils cannot be checked only be legalistic and technical interpretations of law by the judiciary. It is because neither by training nor by their exposure to the complexities of democratic process, judges are equipped to deal with the growing malaise in the actual functioning of political system. Therefore, the activist champions of judicial intervention are encouraging the judiciary to intervene in areas of governance, which are clearly earmarked for elected legislature and political executive of the country.

It is solely for the political executive and democratically-elected legislature to identify organisations or groups which pose a serious threat to the system of democratic governance. This is the reason why political parties have reacted strongly against the Supreme Court judgment of February 4, 2011, where it observed that "membership of a banned organisation will not make a person a criminal unless he resorts to violence".

True, a democratic political system cannot allow any party to crush its political opponents and dissident groups. This is the reason why democracies do not give unlimited power to political executive to impose 'ban' on every non-conformist groups. Hence, it is no one's case that the Government should have a blanket right to declare any group illegal and ban its activities because the party in power can thus target its opponents to remain challenged.

However, the moot question is whether a country, which is the target of gun-wielding terrorist groups, should have a legal arrangement for 'banning' the practitioners of violence against democracy. The recent ruling regarding executive's power to 'ban' violent organisations has highlighted the dangers that are inherent in an over-active judicial system. It is clear that the phenomenon of 'judicial activism and interventionism' cannot be legitimised in blindly because judges can also cross the boundaries laid down by the Constitution of India.

It was not a partisan issue when Prime Minister Manmohan Singh pointed out recently, "while the power of judicial review must be used to enforce accountability, it must never be used to erode the legitimate role assigned to other branches of the Government". He further stated, "this is vitally necessary to preserve the integrity and sanctity of the constitutional scheme premised on the diffusion of sovereign power."

If executive and legislative branches are tempted to extend their jurisdiction beyond the limits laid down by the Constitution, it is for the judiciary to 'control' them and remind them of their limited powers. However, we are witnessing a strange phenomenon where judiciary is enjoying public acclaim by pronouncing judgements on areas of governance where it is not expected to sit as an adjudicator.

The Central Vigilance Commissioner PJ Thomas, under review by the Supreme Court, hit the nail on the head when he said that continuing prosecution of a case does not mean that the 'guilt' has been established because in that case, 153 MPs out of 543 members of the Lok Sabha would have been 'disqualified'. His statement reflects the crucial issue of delay in pronouncing judgements.

Indian judiciary, including the Supreme Court, is known for delaying the dispensation of justice. More than 3 lakh cases are still pending before the Supreme Court. It makes people lose confidence in the judicial system of the country because justice delayed is justice denied. The priority for the Bar and the Bench should be to restore the credibility of the judicial process, not getting involved in issues that would bring them into the limelight.

Judges forget that they need to be respected for their judgments and not for their lengthy moralistic pronouncements.

The former Chief Justice of India PN Bhagwati innovated the system of 'Public Interest Litigation' and the educated elite applauded it as an opportunity to make the political executive more accountable. However, PIL has become quite attractive for publicity-hunting individuals and judges had to limit the admission of PILs by making a distinction between genuine and frivolous PILs.

It is another telling example of judiciary being overburdened by entertaining PILs and not concentrating on the disposal of millions of cases pending for years.

If political executive is losing its legitimacy in the eyes of voters for committing serious acts of omission and commission, then the credibility of judiciary as a dispenser of quick and fair judgement has also been eroded.

The test of a healthy judicial system is that an ordinary and faceless citizen can approach the court for quick justice with minimum expenditure.

—18 February, 2011, The Pioneer

... but Gloating will not Help

The BJP is prematurely celebrating 'victory' by compelling the UPA government to appoint a JPC. The special judge's ruling that Godhra was a 'pre-planned conspiracy' has also heightened its enthusiasm. These two issues are still wide open. It is too early to draw conclusions.

The first thing to note is that the Gujarat riots cannot be delinked from the bandh called by VHP on February 28. The mayhem which followed in March against the Muslims was a direct result. The special court's judgement will undoubtedly be challenged, but more important is the establishment of the Nanavati Commission which maintained that it was a pre-planned conspiracy. The Nanavati Commission's credibility is questionable because the report referred to the conspirators as 'communal Muslims'.

It is not expected of an Hon'ble Judge to identify the conspirators and trouble makers as members of a particular community. The Nanavati Commission was not able to convince the people of its fairness and objectivity. The Justice (retd) UC Banerjee Committee categorically stated that Godhra was an 'accident' and not a 'conspiracy'.

If two inquiry panels arrived at contradictory conclusions, it often leads to doubts over the ability of the nation to find a resolution. The BJP is jumping the gun because the conspiracy bogey suits their agenda. The issue is important because it is a mindset which maintains that 'communal Muslims' hatched a conspiracy to burn Kar Sevaks. The government of Gujarat was helpless when emotions burst and riots followed. It is not only disingenuous to link the burning with its 'consequences' (the riots) because it amounts to absolving the BJP of its failure to take effective action against the rioters.

The BJP's own logic of 'cause-leading-to-consequence' should have made them alert to the possibility of vendetta lynching of Muslims. This is the reason why the Supreme Court directly intervened to investigate the entire series of events of March and April 2002 under its own SIT.

The political class of Gujarat is not ready to confront the rioters. The police functionaries become passive at the suggestion of booking the culprits. It is nobody's argument that Gujarat was the first-ever communal riot incident in India. The defence in favour of Narendra Modi ('why single poor Modi out?') collapses; unlike previous governments that failed to act against communally inspired riots, Modi's failure was deliberate.

If Modi's logic is accepted, the 2G scam can also be dismissed by the Manmohan Singh government because scams are nothing new in India. This country is notorious internationally for its corrupt public figures. Consequently, the BJP must bear the sole responsibility for destroying one whole Parliament session. It cannot hope to gain credibility by adopting different standards for the post-Godhra riots and 2G.

Is India doomed to suffer corruption and communalism because its politicians get away by playing a blame game? The larger question is the total change effected in Indian politics. The first decade of the 21st century has seen every major political party, whether at the central or state level, being proved corrupt. So every political party is responsible for its acts of commission and omission. The Congress was trying to scuttle the issue of corruption by pointing fingers at the BJP government in Karnataka. Should the Congress be allowed to get away with this game? Similarly, the BJP cannot be allowed to shun its duty to provide secular governance. The issue gets dramatised whenever the BJP is attacked because this party's leaders hark back to the 1984 anti-Sikh riots. Should every riot not be condemned? Or should the Congress and the BJP escape their responsibilities by playing the tu-tu-main-main game?

All political parties in power on the basis of one-man-one-vote has to be focussed on the safety and security of life and property of all citizens irrespective of religion. New questions have risen over the role of the judiciary in corruption. The judiciary's neutrality when ruling on communal riots is also an issue today. Every defender of democracy should be extremely worried about this development. It is the role of the political executive and not the judiciary to govern on the basis of supremacy of law. And, any violation of law should be viewed by the Executive with exceptional concern particularly if its own leaders and employees are involved. Amit Shah, a minister in Gujarat, was arrested because the judiciary wanted it. A Raja has been arrested because the CBI was being supervised by the judiciary and therefore the premier investigating agency had no option.

Judicial activism and interventionism, which is growing in India, can lead to oligarchy and undermine democracy. If judges are seen managing the affairs of governments by creating SITs or ordering the

CBI to report progress, every lover of democracy should be embarrassed. In Pakistan it was the judges who presided over the fall of the Musharraf dictatorship. The principle of power separation and balance of power in the Indian Constitution seems to have been lost on the political class of India today.

—26 February, 2011, The Pioneer

Maoists Bereft of Marxist Ideology

The abduction of functionaries of the state or the killing of security personnel or the boastful declaration of the liberated Red Corridor may garner enough publicity for gun-wielding Maoists but such strategies will definitely not help in achieving their goal of social transformation.

The society has changed a lot since the first Maoist uprising took place at Naxalbari in West Bengal in mid 1960s. New social challenges have emerged in the country over the last 50 years. The Maoist leadership has failed to demystify the complex and contradictory dialectics of social reality because leaders of the Maoist movement—be it Kanu Sanyal and Charu Majumdar during mid-1960s or Kishenji of today—have kept themselves away from the theory and praxis of Karl Marx.

Since Maoists in India do not really follow the philosophy of Karl Marx, they have neither analysed nor understood the inherent flaws that characterised the Telangana People's Armed Struggle led by the Communist Party of India just after India got independence. The Communist Party of India abandoned the path of armed struggle because it realised after the withdrawal of peasants' struggle in Telangana that armed revolutionary struggles are completely counterproductive, even redundant, in India because people have accepted the politics of ballot.

Indians, since they actively participate in the electoral process, believe that democratically elected leaders will bring about social changes in the country. Maoists, on the other hand, have failed to understand that the level of social consciousness of the people, including the deprived, have undergone a sea change because of the ongoing democratic process.

Unlike Maoist leaders who prefer to fight guerilla wars, leaders of the Communist Party of India and the Communist Party of India (Marxists) have joined the mainstream politics, got democratically elected, formed Governments in West Bengal, Tripura and Kerala and have impacted national politics by their presence in Parliament.

The Governments ruled by Communist parties have successfully undertaken land reforms and restructuring of agrarian class relations. The Communist movement in India has brought together the peasantry, the urban working class and the lower middle-class intelligentsia on the same platform and have successfully launched struggles for better service conditions of workers and progressive legislation on social security.

This underscores the fact that Indian democracy provides enough political space for launching struggles for the rights of different social groups, including the proletariat. Therefore, the basic failure of Maoist leadership lies in the fact that they have completely misread the implications of democracy.

Further, Maoists are wrong in believing that struggles for the rights of tribals can be successful without a broad social platform. This is particularly true in a democracy like India, which is socially, politically and culturally diverse and where forming alliances with multiple social groups to achieve common goals is the norm. Precisely, this is the reason why Maosists lack any broad mass support.

Since Maoists do not Follow Karl Marx, they have not learnt the basic tenet of revolution—that lessons have to be learnt from every failed social struggle. Karl Marx declared in 1848 that the spectre of communism haunts Europe. But after its failure, he critically re-examined his theory on revolution.

Further, Maoists in India must realise that following Mao Tse-tung's ideology will not help because a Long March, the central event in the Chinese revolution, is not possible in India as the Indian society and state are fundamentally different from that of Mao's China. Left parties in Indonesia, Malaysia, Thailand, Philippines, Burma and other countries, who are influenced by the Maoist ideology, have failed to achieve any success because they wanted to replicate Mao's revolution without understanding a simple fact that revolutions cannot be copied. Same holds true for Maoists in India.

In India, political leaders, since they are elected by the people, can claim legitimately that they represent the people and work for them. A competitive democratic politics provides an opportunity for political alternatives to contest against one another by mobilising social constituencies. Alterative levels of social consciousness can emerge and have emerged through democratic social struggles. But Indian Maoists are adopting short cuts to revolution because launching democratic struggle for people's rights requires a very sustained and patient political activity.

That Maoists in India are victims of serious limitations of their own theory was exposed during the recent 'hostage crisis' in the State of Odisha. The gun-wielding Maoists have witnessed how the poor tribals in Malkangiri turned hostile because of their deep sense of anger against the abduction of a popular district Collector. Maoists have to accept the serious limitations of politics of gun, in a functioning democracy like India. In fact, because of their slogan that 'revolution flows from the barrel of a gun', majority of landless agricultural labourers, marginal farmers, millions of deprived in rural and urban India have kept themselves away from Maoists ideology.

—4 March, 2011, The Pioneer

Unravelling Coalitions

The forthcoming assembly elections in Kerala, Tamil Nadu, Puducherry, West Bengal and Assam are likely to exercise a direct impact on the future directions of the Congress-led UPA government at the Centre. The stakes for the Congress in these elections are very high not only because it is an important political player in these states but also because the DMK and the Trinamool Congress (TMC), troublesome constituents of the UPA, are contesting the assembly elections in alliance with the Congress.

The process of distribution of seats in these two states has clearly revealed that Congress, as a junior coalition partner of the DMK and the TMC, had to bargain very hard for the number of constituencies where it was allowed to contest by the regional Big Brothers.

The story of Assam and Kerala is different because in these two states, the Congress is a leading political player and despite this fact, the party's performance in these two states does not have any direct meaning for the functioning of the UPA government. The DMK and the TMC are contesting the elections not only with a view to form their own state governments, but they also want to strengthen their position in these two states so that they can renegotiate their actual relationship with the Congress at the Centre.

India is experiencing a type of politics where coalition governments at the Centre are inter-locked with coalitions at the state level and in the context of this new political equilibrium, the political role of every major regional party is not confined only to the boundaries of its own specific region.

A significant fact is that the assembly elections are also experiencing the politics of 'coalition versus coalition' and all major state political players have to form a 'coalition' to win an election. If coalitions from above and coalitions from below have become a reality of India's 'tripolar political system', it should lead to a system of governance, both at the Centre and states, which is accommodative of different social interests and demands, and extremism in politics should become redundant because coalition politics is based on the principle of consensus.

This is only part of the story. Coalitional model of politics both at the central and state government levels has not led to a system of good governance based on the principle of accommodation of different, even conflicting, interests and demands of separate groups pulls the coalition government in different directions.

When Prime Minister Manmohan Singh was put on the defensive on the role of DMK telecommunications minister A Raja in the 2G scam, he took refuge behind the 'compulsions of a coalition' government. Corruption, maladministration and misgovernance are tolerated so that coalition partners do not walk out. The form is of a coalition government but the real substance is that every coalition partner operates in an autonomous manner.

Further, corruption in governments has increased because every coalition partner collects money for his/her own political group and every ally in the coalition is busy in separately accumulating funds. This is the reason for the Election Commission insisting on 'the filing of an affidavit' by every contesting candidate mentioning his 'income status' and income tax officials have been mobilised to monitor the role of money power during these elections. Politics has become a lucrative business because even a leader of a 'mini political shop' can become a minister if he joins the winning party.

The ongoing process of fragmentation and proliferation of parties and personality-based groups has created a situation where coalitions at the Centre or the state levels have become a motley collection where nothing binds them together except the logic of power for the sake of personal benefits. Mamata has fielded candidates who are not a product of grassroots politics and because her party does not have any manifesto or programme for governance, these actors, actresses, retired IAS or IPS or a Ficci general secretary are all bound together on a negative platform of forming an anti-communist government.

Can such a coalition provide a meaningful and purposeful government in West Bengal? All the five state assembly elections are a contest where the dominant factor among the political players is to capture political power and maintain the status quo. Parties do have to win elections for governance, but the issue is that these coalitions at the state levels have not given any new pro-people message.

But the coalition system shall continue as an integral feature of a multi-polar party/political system of India. The Indian political journey of minimal firm consensus system of governance is not on the agenda at the present, irrespective of the elections.

—26 March, 2011, The Economic Times

Alliances of Convenience, not Ideology

The Assembly elections coming up next month in six States are crucial not only for the Congress but also for regional political players like the Trinamool Congress, the DMK, the AIADMK and the Asom Gana Parishad. On the one hand, every State has political specificities of its own, on the other, every State is witnessing contests between multi-party coalitions.

With regional political parties emerging stronger in Indian politics over the past two decades, the Union Government, irrespective of the party in power, has become dependent on the support of regional players. They throw their weight around depending on the strength of their representation in Parliament and the national party in power—be it the BJP or the Congress—has to oblige for fear of losing the majority in the House. On the other hand, the national parties piggyback their regional allies to capture power in the States. Hence, seat-sharing becomes significant as it all adds up to coalition arithmetic.

The elections in Tamil Nadu and West Bengal are of utmost significance because if the DMK and the Trinamool Congress lose the electoral battle, their bargaining power at the Centre will diminish. The Congress and other allies of the UPA will become more assertive. The opposite holds true in the event of the DMK and the TMC emerging victorious as both parties without doubt will demand greater share of power at the Centre.

Seat distribution among allies, thus, is a serious political exercise as all parties are engaged in defending their political spaces and constituencies. The Congress has been involved in prolonged negotiations with the DMK on seat-sharing as it wants to strengthen its political identity in Tamil Nadu. The Congress is bargaining hard with TMC chief Mamata Banerjee for a larger share of seats in West Bengal because if it can win a sizeable number of seats it can stake claims to be a part of the Government after the election.

Further, the Congress knows how the DMK and the Trinamool Congress have turned their Ministries into personal fiefdom and often disregard the Prime Minister's instructions. If these two parties are given a long rope in the Assembly elections, they will become unmanageable after capturing power in the States. Hence, it wants to checkmate the arm-twisting tactics of its allies by sharing power in the States.

Even minor players in Tamil Nadu are engaged in positioning themselves as future partners in the governing coalition. The DMK has won over Mr Anbumani Ramadoss's Vanniyar caste-based regional outfit, Pattalı Makkal Katchi by offering 29 Assembly seats (the PMK sacrificed two seats from its initial quota of 31 to the Congress to resolve the seat crisis) and a Rajya Sabha seat. The AIADMK, on its part, has roped in actor-turned-politician Mr Vijayakanth's DMDK by alotting 41 seats.

The stakes are also high in Assam where the Congress is fighting anti-incumbency while seeking a third-term in power. The Congress is being challenged by the Asom Gana Parishad-led alliance. Asom Gana Parishad gained prominence in Assam politics by leading the Anti-Foreigner Movement from 1979 to 1985. The issue of illegal Bangladeshi migrants has always engaged the attention of the people of Assam and the inadequacy of the Anti-Foreigner Act in checking the infiltration of Bangladeshis has always been a sore point.

In Kerala, the Congress-led United Democratic Front is likely to come back to power defeating the Left Democratic Front. The CPI(M)'s move to remove Mr VS Achuthanandan from leading the party can adversely affect the LDF's prospects as he is the only man capable of salvaging the LDF from a poll disaster. Further, Kerala has always witnessed anti-incumbency with the LDF and the UDF taking turns in forming the Government every five years.

Electoral contest in all these sates has a dual reality. On the one hand, the partners in a coalition will like to maximise their own strength at the cost of other partners, on the other, it will be a battle between two coalitions. This duality of coalitional politics at the state level explains the tug-of-war over seat-sharing.

Another reality of coalition versus coalition electoral contests is that every partner of a coalition concentrates only on its own social constituency and mobilises its own resources and cadre though all partners are supposed to help each other in winning polls. In fact, this is the reason why money power has become so important in politics. No major party leading a coalition shares its financial resources with its so-called allies who are left to fend for themselves. It is because every partner in a coalition wants to maintain its separate identity and maximise its strength.

The only model of united coalition is the alliance of Left parties in West Bengal, Kerala and Tripura. All other coalitions are temporary marriages of convenience. Tamil Nadu is a case in point. The AIADMK and the DMK have been constantly changing their allies every election. Mr Ramdoss's PMK was with the AIADMK in the Lok Sabha election of 2009 but it has walked over to the DMK before the Assembly election of 2011.

—18 March, 2011, The Pioneer

Voters are Conscious of Their Rights

Anna Hazare got instant all-India fame when he successfully launched a campaign for the enactment of the Jan Lok Pal Bill by Parliament. But publicity has made him a reckless critic of democratic India's electoral process which is no doubt flawed and corrupt. It was fantastic non-sense for Mr Hazare to observe on April 10, 2011 that an 'ordinary voter does not have awareness... They do not understand the value of their vote.'

As if this was not enough, he went on to assert that 'if I fight elections I will lose my deposit. I don't have money to buy up voter and buy them alcohol or a sari.' It was not unexpected that political leaders like Mr LK Advani, Mr Digvijay Singh, Mr Mulayam Singh Yadav *et al* would publicly state that Mr Hazare was wrong to paint every elected representative in black and had opted to condemn the whole political system in a blanket manner.

Not only this, Mr Hazare's ill-founded general censure of the democratic political process led many tall leaders to ask questions about the very legitimacy of the 'unelected and unrepresentative' individuals, who along with Mr Hazare, launched a movement for the enactment of the Jan Lok Pal Bill.

How can elected representatives, even in a completely imperfect democracy, accept the pre-eminent role of the 'unelected' in public policy formulation processes and supplant the elected Government and Parliament in India? It will be an unempirical statement to make that the role of black money and involvement of criminals is not a reality of the political-electoral process. However, it shows a high level of ignorance on Mr Hazare's behalf when he claims that the Indian voters are not politically conscious and are solely guided by petty temptations when exercising their very valuable right of vote during the elections.

A few facts may be mentioned to substantiate the argument that the illiterate, the poor, and the wretched have shown a highly developed political sense while participating in elections. First, a large section of Indians have exercised their precious right to vote under the shadow of gun wielding militants, secessionists and terrorists. Elections for Panchayati Raj Institutions were held in two phases in Jammu and Kashmir under the dictates of separatists who had called for a 'boycott of elections'. Still in this atmosphere of fear, 78 to 82 per cent of Kashmiris decided to vote. Only cynics and vulgar armed-chair elite can ignore the active participation of citizens even in State like Jammu and Kashmir where militancy is at its peak. In Assam, the State Assembly election held in April brought more than 70 per cent men and women to the polling booths despite a segment of disgruntled gun-wielding ULFA cadre continuing to terrorise voters. How can one dismiss such conscious voters in States and regions that are witnessing 'abnormal' political situations? Fear was conspicuous by its absence among voters when they decided to punish Mrs Indira Gandhi for her authoritarian Emergency regime in 1977?

Second, elections in India have become highly competitive and every major or minor party and leader is on his tenterhooks because of fear of punishment by the voter. If Indian voter is not conscious of his rights, the country would have been ruled by only one party and one party dictatorship would have been the order of the day.

Voters have changed the political map of India and by electing or rejecting parties, a system of multi-polar democracy has emerged where all-India national parties have to co-exist and compete with regional parties. The outcome of the Assembly elections of Kerala and Tamil Nadu is unpredictable because of unexpected heavy voter turnout. Is Mr M Karunnadhi's DMK, with huge financial resources at its command, sure about electoral victory? Election studies have shown that large number of voters accept money or other goodies from every candidate or party and make promises to vote the party candidate but in reality the secret ballot is secret and the voter has learnt to milch every party.

Thirdly, a significant fact of electoral politics is that it is the poor, deprived and struggling labouring classes that are in the forefront of participation during elections and it is the comfortable metropolitan middle class comprising professional businessmen and others are the ones who stay one. Political parties have to undertake a lot of effort to bring the so-called highly educated strata of society to the 'polling booth' for voting during the elections.

It is an insult to the Indian democracy to maintain, or even suggest, that the Indian voter is not 'conscious' of his right to vote because serious election studies disprove such condemnatory statements made by armed-chair, candle-light protestors belonging to the middle classes of metropolitan cities.

—29 April, 2011, The Pioneer

Political Funding: Need vs. Greed

Democratic legitimacy of elected political representatives seems to be eroded to the extent that a person of the status of the Chief Election Commissioner SY Quraishi, on the basis of his latest experience of recent state assembly elections , made a public statement on April 12 that 'there is large-scale electoral corruption. The role of criminals and money power is rampant.'

Indeed, the democratic electoral process has been completely polluted by political parties and their leaders who are prepared to adopt every conceivable corrupt practice to win elections. In spite of strict vigilance exercised by the EC on unfair and criminal activities indulged in by the parties and contesting candidates during the elections, these malpractices have not come to an end. Hence, there is an urgent need for addressing this problem and an important step in this direction is to examine the institutional mechanisms which have been created by democratic countries in the industrial capitalist West for not only checking but even eliminating the practices which pollute and delegitimise democratic elections.

The late 18th and 19th century history of elections in the US and England shows that the offices of elective representative assemblies, Parliament or Congress were 'bought' by rich sections of nobility, the aristocracy or, in the case of the US, the owners of large landed estates and slave labour. This system of purchase of elective offices by wealthy people was described as 'pocket-borough' in England where money was openly offered and accepted for electing a representative and American historians have described the early phase of their democracy as being controlled by 'robber barons' who had wealth and slaves.

A very prestigious publication, *Money in Politics Handbook*, enlightens the practices which have been adopted by various democratic countries to ensure the elimination of unaccounted money spent by individual candidates or parties to influence voters by purchasing votes. The first important step in making politics clean is that every individual candidate for any elective office should 'disclose' the source of donations received by him for participating in the elections. Laws have been passed in some democratic countries to bind every candidate to 'disclose' his sources of funds for elections. The justification for disclosure laws was summed up by the Prime Minister of Thailand as 'corrupt people fear information. What the government knows, the people should know'.

This led USAID to sponsor a survey conducted by the International Foundation of Election Systems with a purpose to find the status of 'Disclosure Laws' in 118 countries. North America and Europe, which began their democratic journey with complete corruption in their electoral process, have achieved 80-100 per cent compliance of the Public Disclosure Report by candidates. Further, donations are collected not only by individual candidate but also political parties and the task will be half-done if candidates, and not parties, are put under legal obligation for public disclosure of their income and expenses and also names of donors of parties. Political parties in a democracy are a public institution and many countries have stringent laws for auditing the accounts of parties and individual candidates.

For example, Western Australia has a comprehensive law of 'Offences under the Electoral Act, 1907, or 'Offences under the Electoral (Political Finance) Regulations 1996' and neither candidates nor parties can evade these laws except if they are prepared to face stringent punishment amounting to hefty fines or imprisonment. Why cannot India frame laws for disclosure of political finance and why cannot election activity, including sources of donation, be made transparent? The source of corruption in elections is the 'secrecy' practiced by every party and leader about the sources of their funds for elections.

It is a well-known fact that every party has a 'loyal and faithful' fund collector who is accountable only to the supreme leader or dynasty-based regional bosses. India has taken an important first step that candidates contesting elections have to declare their personal financial and property interests, but this is not enough because every candidate or party gets funds from private promoters for elections. Parliament should create a separate constitutional autonomous authority of an auditor-general to ensure disclosure of the sources of funds which are invested during the elections. The system of election petitions has completely failed to check the rot in Indian polity and the credibility of democratically elected representatives can be restored by appointing an ombudsman for acting as a watchdog of the parties. Unfortunately, in India, need and greed for funds has become interchangeable and this has polluted and corrupted the electoral system. It's time to change that.

—30 April, 2011, The Economic Times

... but isn't the Constitution Supreme?

Nothing short of a revolution can take away the lawmakers' right to write and pass laws. Anna Hazare is pushing the envelope too hard and it's time he decided to save himself for another fight, some other day.

The first issue is that Anna Hazare and Company is trying to legitimise their fast unto death by misappropriating Mohandas Karamchand Gandhi. But Gandhi never shied from entering into negotiations. His moral stature was proved when he offered to talk even to Mohammad Ali Jinnah till the last moment to avoid the partition of India. Gandhi offered Jinnah the prime ministership of united India.

Gandhi's Satyagraha, unlike the circus of Hazare and his friends, was based on solid foundations. The context was very different than the present one. Gandhi led mass movements in stages to make Indians conscious of their right to freedom against oppressive, repressive and racist colonial rule. Not only this, unlike Anna's lieutenants like Arvind Kejriwal, Kiran Bedi or Swami Agnivesh, Gandhi's aides— Nehru, Patel, etc.—spent long terms in prison. Their sacrifices in the cause of freedom can hardly be matched. Anna's comrades cannot occupy that kind of moral space. The right of only Magsaysay awardees to be members of a government-appointed joint committee for deliberating on the Jan Lokpal Bill is most ridiculous. Further, it is not a question of setting up a joint committee with a view to carrying out negotiations on the principle of give and take, Anna has already operationalised the role which would be performed by the Lokpal. In the process, the Lokpal would emerge as a supra State with its own parliament and constitution.

There is nothing wrong in saying that the Lokpal should have jurisdiction over politicians, officials and judges. But Anna is making the astounding suggestion that the probe into allegations of corruption should be completed within one year. Then he demands that trials based on such probes should be completed within one year. This is the crux of the issue. The Indian Constitutional and legal system attaches highest importance to the rule of law and it is the fundamental right of every citizen to file an appeal against any verdict. Anna does not seem to accept this basic principle of innocent till proved guilty. What is the guarantee that the draconian procedure suggested by him will not lead to arbitrary bodies lacking checks and balances? It should be noted that the tone and tenor of the agitators assembled around Anna are creating a climate of hatred towards our democratic profile. A shadow has been cast over democracy. When Anna publicly identified Sharad Pawar as "corrupt minister", what followed resembled the functioning of a kangaroo court. How can anybody be held guilty and make public announcements of this nature?

Further, the media, both audio and visual, as well as political parties which are explicitly or implicitly reveling in Anna's tamasha because the issue is not the Manmohan Singh government, but actually the place of elected parliamentarians in the democratic system. It is the job of the lawmakers to make laws, including the Jan Lokpal Bill, and the Constitution does not make a provision for wannabe Mahatmas to sit at the high table with Ministers and legislators in the writing and passing of laws.

Of course, there is scope for consultation with experts of all hues, including social mobilisers like Anna Hazare. But whatever the corruption situation, there is no "revolution" necessary right now for the purpose of making our anti-corruption law workable. Moreover, expecting the government to give a 'guarantee' even before going to Parliament with the proposal, smacks of mobocracy. No elected government can afford to ignore Parliament.

As much as it is the right of the government to frame laws, so too is the Opposition mandated to seek finetuning and insertion of checks and balances. There are Consultative Committees, Select Committees, Standing Committees and Review Commissions mandated by the Constitution to ensure that the people's right to a clear law is evolved. Granted there is always scope for improvement.

Many laws and passed only to be amended in the following session of Parliament. That is another beauty of the democratic system. Anna Hazare seems to be intent on turning all this upside down just to prove a point that winners of awards presented by foreign governments know better than elected representatives of the Indian people, The young and constantly role-defining TV media of India has played a dangerous role in the whole affair.

They seem to be obsessed so much with Tehrir Square being replicated in India that they have thrown all norms to the winds. They fail to realise that it is impossible to have revolutions of the kind seen in Tunisia, Egypt, Libya and even earlier in countries in the former East Bloc in functioning democracies like India. Here, apart from a vibrant—even if corrupt—polity, we have other institutions which can be approached to secure for the common man his basic rights.

Anna Hazare rightly points to corruption in the judiciary. It is nobody's case that all judges are above board. But who can deny that judicial activism has on several occasions brought an arrogant Executive down by a couple of notches. Anna Hazare should therefore save himself for another fight. He has done yeoman's service by rallying national energy around the cause of corruption-free governance. Now that he has set the ball rolling, he should prepare himself for the other struggles for which the people of India desperately need leadership.

—*9 April, 2011, The Pioneer*

New Challenges for Communists

Communist parties have suffered serious electoral setbacks in the state assembly elections of Kerala and West Bengal, but it can be asserted that the communists can definitely make a comeback and play a crucial role in Indian politics. The audio-visual and print media has pronounced hasty and unwarranted judgements about the future of communist parties.

It is nothing new because the Congress party had also been written off when its monopoly of power over the central and state governments had come to an inglorious end in the post-Rajiv Gandhi phase of politics. The CPI(M)-led Left Front in West Bengal had won 235 assembly seats out of 294 and its share of vote was 50.18 per cent in the elections of 2006; in the 2011 elections it has won 62 seats and its share of votes is 41 per cent and the CPI(M)'s share alone is 40 per cent. The social support base of a party is always known on the basis of its share of votes. Hence, the task before the communists of West Bengal is to win over the 9 per cent of its support base and the analytical question is to identify the causes for the withdrawal of voters' support.

Communists had made every effort to face the challenge posed by Mamata Banerjee's platform of paribortan or change by following the strategy of 'Renewal and Young Blood' as pronounced by Biman Bose of the CPI(M). The Left Front did not nominate 91 sitting MLAs and some ministers, and it projected 150 new faces and 46 women candidates for the elections of 2011. Why is it that Mamata's paribortan carried greater conviction with the voters, including a sizeable number of traditional communist supporters? The electoral defeat of the LDF in Kerala was based on a self-goal because of factional fights like Pinarayi Vijayan versus VS Achutanandan.

The LDF, in 2011, secured 68 seats and its share of votes was 45 per cent, only 3 per cent less than the winning Congress-led UDF, which won 72 seats. The Kerala CPI(M) handed electoral victory to the Congress on a platter because till the end it kept fighting with Achutanandan , an unquestioned mass leader in the state. Prakash Karat, after the polit bureau meeting of May 16, stated that there was a 'disconnect' with the voters of Bengal who had been 'alienated' from the party.

AB Bardhan, a veteran communist leader, went a step forward and stated that electoral defeat was the result of 'arrogance' of the leaders. These explanations only focus attention on the 'style of functioning' of the leadership. Such 'self-criticism' is quite insufficient to revive and revitalise the communist movement in India. First, the communists in West Bengal had been on the backfoot in the panchayat elections, the Lok Sabha elections and municipal elections of 2008, 2009 and 2010 and it is difficult to accept that the party leadership was not getting proper signals from these electoral setbacks.

Second, the larger issue is that the communists were retreating from the political scene because after rural development programmes—they simply could not grapple with the new challenge brought about by social changes taking place in West Bengal in particular and India in general. It is a simple fact to state that at the end of the first decade of the 21st century, a relatively backward West Bengal came to coexist with other regions of the country which were experiencing rapid industrial growth along with the emergence of centres of the New Economy, especially telecommunications , petrochemical industries, *et al.*

But West Bengal's hesitant steps to attract big industrialists like Tata and also launching of mega Haldia project ended in a tragedy on the issue of land acquisition. Karl Marx clearly stated that 'society is real and the individual is a reality' and this social dialectics of reality should always be the guiding factor in the thinking processes of the communists.

AB Bardhan has alerted the communists on ignoring the new social reality and in an interview on May 18, he said that 'one thing the Left has underestimated is that a great middle class has grown up in the last few decades... it moulds public opinion' and he went on to state that the Left must 'confront the fact that having lost is influence in the old middle class, it has not yet found a way to talk to the new.' The real issue, thus, is the Left's incapacity to remain alive to the changing social dialectics of India and the pattern of changes in the levels of aspirations of different classes in the country.

The communists also have to confront the forces of communal fascism represented by the Sangh Parivar. Instead of wasting energies on creating the Third Front and following afailed policy of equidistance from the Congress and BJP, they should catch the bull by the horns and launch struggles against the divisive policy of religious separatism of the Sangh

Parivar. These are the ideological and political tasks before the communists, and if performed well, the ideology has a future in a country of mass deprivation and acute poverty.

The communists face the test of reviving and revitalising their movement The real challenge for them is to stay alive to the changing social dynamics of the nation To remain relevant, the communists would also have to confront divisive politics.

—28 May, 2011, The Economic Times

Is it New Satyagrah or Mobicracy

The first issue is that Baba Ramdev, like Anna Hazare and Company before him, is trying to legitimise the instrument of fast unto death by misappropriating Mohandas Karamchand Gandhi. But Gandhi never shied from entering into negotiations. His moral stature was proved when he offered to talk even to Mohammad Ali Jinnah till the last moment to avoid the partition of India. Gandhi offered Jinnah the prime ministership of united India.

Gandhi's *Satyagrah,* unlike the proposed circus of Baba Ramdev, was based on solid foundations. The context was very different than the present one. Gandhi led mass movements in stages to make Indians conscious of their right to freedom against oppressive, repressive and racist colonial rule. Not only this, unlike Anna's lieutenants like Arvind Kejriwal, Kiran Bedi or Swami Agnivesh, Gandhi's aides—Nehru, Patel, etc.—spent long terms in prison. Their sacrifices in the cause of freedom can hardly be matched. Anna's comrades cannot occupy that kind of moral space.

The right of only Magsaysay awardees to be members of a government-appointed joint committee for deliberating on the Jan Lokpal Bill is most ridiculous. Further, it is not a question of setting up a joint committee with a view to carrying out negotiations on the principle of give and take, Anna has already operationalised the role which would be performed by the Lokpal. In the process, the Lokpal would emerge as a supra State with its own parliament and constitution.

There is nothing wrong in saying that the Lokpal should have jurisdiction over politicians, officials and judges. But Anna is making the astounding suggestion that the probe into allegations of corruption should be completed within one year. Then he demands that trials based on such probes should be completed within one year. This is the crux of the issue. The Indian constitutional and legal system attaches highest importance to the rule of law and it is the fundamental right of every citizen to file an appeal against any verdict. Anna does not seem to accept this basic principle of innocent till proved guilty.

What is the guarantee that the draconian procedure suggested by him will not lead to arbitrary bodies lacking checks and balances? It should be noted that the tone and tenor of the agitators assembled around Anna are creating a climate of hatred towards our democratic profile. A shadow has been cast over democracy. When Anna publicly identified Sharad Pawar as "corrupt minister", what followed resembled the functioning of a kangaroo court. How can anybody be held guilty and make public announcements of this nature?

Further, the media, both and audio-visual, as well as political parties which are explicitly or implicitly reveling in Anna's tamasha because the issue is not the Manmohan Singh government, but actually the place of elected parliamentarians in the democratic system. It is the job of the lawmakers to make laws, including the Jan Lokpal Bill, and the Constitution does not make a provision for wannabe Mahatmas to sit at the high table with Ministers and legislators in the writing and passing of laws. Of course, there is scope for consultation with experts of all hues, including social mobilisers like Anna. But whatever the corruption situation, there is no "revolution" necessary right now for the purpose of making our anti-corruption law workable.

Moreover, expecting the government to give a 'guarantee' even before going to Parliament with the proposal, smacks of mobocracy. No elected government can afford to ignore Parliament. As much as it is the right of the government to frame laws, so too is the Opposition mandated to seek fine tuning and insertion of checks and balances. There are Consultative Committees, Select Committees, Standing Committees and Review Commissions mandated by the Constitution to ensure that the people's right to a clear law is evolved. Granted there is always scope for improvement. Many laws and passed only to be amended in the following session of Parliament.

That is another beauty of the democratic system. Anna Hazare seems to be intent on turning all this upside down just to prove a point that winners of awards presented by foreign governments know better than elected representatives of the Indian people. The young and constantly role defining TV media of India has played a dangerous role in the whole affair. They seem to be obsessed so much with Tehrir Square being replicated in India that they have thrown all norms to the winds. They fail to realise that it is impossible to have revolutions of the kind seen in Tunisia, Egypt, Libya and even earlier in countries in the former East Bloc in functioning democracies like India. Here, apart from a vibrant—even if corrupt—polity, we have other institutions which can be approached to secure for the common man his basic rights. Anna Hazare rightly points to corruption in the judiciary. It is nobody's case that all judges are above board. But who can deny that judicial activism has on several occasions brought an arrogant Executive down by a couple of notches.

Baba Ramdev should therefore save himself for another fight. He has done yeoman's service by rallying national energy around the cause of corruption-free governance. Now that he has set the ball rolling, he should prepare himself for the other struggles for which the people of India desperately need leadership.

—4 June, 2011, The Pioneer

Trivialising the Nation's Political Process

While presenting to the voters its list of achievements over the past two years, the Congress led-UPA regime at the Centre said that it had achieved economic growth, increased the number of primary schools and expanded the National Rural Health Mission which now reaches to 264 districts in the country, and invested sizeable public funds in the agricultural sector and infrastructure for development. Further in its 74 page report to the people on May 22, 2011, Congress president Sonia Gandhi asserted that "transparency, accountability and probity are at the very heart of our governance." Finally, with great fanfare the UPA leadership, on its second anniversary, declared that it is determined to fight corruption in public life.

The point however is that it has always been assumed that an elected Government is capable of providing 'clean' administration. Therefore it was rather unusual when the UPA regime had to convince the public that it will provide a corruption-free and clean administration. This is because the UPA regime has completely lost its credibility and must now convince the people that they deserve good governance.

Towards that extent, the Government now, under the direction of the Supreme Court, has CBI Special Courts sentencing the high and mighty associated with the Union Government on charges of robbing the national treasury while performing their duties as public functionaries. This points to an unusual public show of commitment by a Government of the day towards ensuring that it is undertaking every effort possible to eradicate the evil of corruption in public life that has been promoted by its own ministers, bureaucrats, leaders and allies in Government.

Clearly, the Congress-led UPA regime at the Centre is completely on the defensive here. It will also not be out of place to state that it is the Opposition parties that have exposed the proverbial skeletons in the UPA cupboard with regard to scams and corruption scandals. Consequently, today the UPA's corrupt nature has become a talking point for the voters on the streets of India.

People have now literally come out on the streets to express their anger.

This has also given public figures like Anna Hazare or Baba Ramdev the opportunity to successfully mobilise large sections of society on the basis of the anti-corruption agenda which caught the nation's attention.

However, the issue at hand is not the role or the popularity of these public mobilisers. Instead, the focus should be on the 'mobilised,' i.e. those who have come out to express their resentment against corrupt political leaders abusing their power. Obviously, the common man feels that he has been cheated and the trust he had reposed in his elected representative has been completely betrayed.

It is however a matter of great concern that the Opposition did not feel it necessary to pursue the anti-corruption agenda after raising the issue in Parliament. Why did the Opposition not organise a mass agitation on this burning issue? Why did Anna Hazare and Baba Ramdev have to jump in to the fray?

Ideally, this fight should have been led by the Opposition which in a parliamentary democracy is the original watchdog of public interests. It is the Opposition's primary responsibility is to keep the Government on its toes and when necessary mobilise public opinion against acts of omission and commission indulged in by the Government.

The Opposition should have been the torch bearer of the anti-corruption agenda. With the support of civil society, they should have compelled the Government to create a strong legal framework for bringing the guilty to the book. The enactment of legislation to curb corruption or bring back Indian money stashed away in safe havens should have been on top of the Opposition agenda. Now, if the Government was not responsive, the Opposition would have been completely within its rights to mobilise public opinion against the ruling party.

But how the Opposition could hand over their legitimate role and duty to private individuals, no matter how well-meaning they are, is beyond comprehension. This is particularly worrying because it is entirely possibly that those who are in the Opposition today may become the ruling party after the next general elections and then the new Opposition will follow the precedents set by those who held the same positions earlier. As a result, elected representatives would have handed over their political space to non-elected "eminent people" who are not accountable to either public or Parliament. Just like by creating the National Advisory Council Ms Sonia Gandhi has established a super cabinet in the process made a laughing stock of the Prime Minister Manmohan Singh's cabinet, the Opposition too stands equally guilty of 'outsourcing' the its task to self appointed 'wise men'.

It must also be said that Mr Singh's Government is also not without fault. Instead of constituting a Joint Committee with non-elected individuals to draft the Lokpal Bill, Mr Singh should have arranged to have in-depth consultation with the Opposition as well as other elected representatives. After all, in every democracy issues of governance are ultimately discussed, debated and resolved by the country's elected representatives. It is a tragedy that today a democratically elected Government in India has now completely surrendered its state authority to a small group of self-appointed crusaders.

—10 June, 2011, The Pioneer

Isn't Corruption Endemic to all Democracies?

The logic of Parliamentary electoral politics is very clear that political parties cannot do without, in fact they "need" finances for their activities, especially for maintaining their organisational network throughout the country. Unfortunately in India, the distinction between "need" and "greed" has been blurred and this is why without any exception, the all-India parties as well as regional parties are involved in wanton accumulation of funds through brazen misuse and abuse of power when they are both in government and opposition.

It may surprise readers to hear that even Opposition parties are caught up in this game. It always happens that a party which is in the Opposition at the Centre, has quite a few State governments under its belt. Again, a state-level Opposition party invariably has a few panchayat or district bodies in its control. So, "devolution of power", which is toasted by the *jholawalla* circuit of Delhi, is actually a macabre operation. Money is now made not only to line a State/central minister's pocket, but also to meet quotas set by the treasurer of the State unit of his party. The State treasurer, in turn, has got to respond to the national treasurer's demands—higher the level, more obscene the requirement. Therefore, "power to the people" has become an empty slogan. It is high time we admitted that more the levels of governance, greater the chance of misuse. And it is happening in a rampant way in India.

So, we have a situation today where the entire edifice of our democracy is standing on weak ground. With coalition governments becoming more the system than exception, newer and newer demands are made on public moneys. Back in the days when big parties won elections by huge sweeps, industrialists and traders saw no need to carry briefcases to leaders of smaller parties. A small number of parties, at the most four or five, had to be kept all over the country. But now every coalition partner, even parties having only one seat, has got to be kept in good humour. Not only that, one is never sure which one-MP or one-MLA party will make or break a government next month. So, giant corporations have begun employing specialists whose only work is to identify politicians for bribing.

It should be remembered that democracies everywhere are corrupt.

No democracy is free of the malaise of corruption. We celebrate democracy not because it is the best form of government, but only because it is preferable to despotism, martial law, fascism, communism, etc. In the so-called "other countries" of western democracy corruption occurs on a very big scale, but it is not as widespread as in India. In Britain, historians on corruption in democracy have alerted us to the past when there existed institutions called "pocket boroughs" which were actually "rotten boroughs". Under that system, votes were openly bought by those seriously in the running for seats in the House of Commons.

The worst case scenario was manifested in the United States where "Robber Barons" would steal the ballot. Much water has flown since then. In every western democracy, the very roots of public life are seized by corruption. Though effective legal structures have been put in place for the conduct of free, fair and sleaze-free elections, there is still vast scope for hanky panky which, doubtless, are exploited. Without labouring this point, the lesson from the western experience is that without initiating similar, drastic electoral reforms India cannot hope to win credibility for its democratic institutions.

The Indian political class, irrespective of ideological pretensions and pronouncements, has shown little respect for the reform proposals introduced by every chief election commissioner over the past 60 years. It is not without reason that the present CEC, Mr Qureshi, resorted to using officials from Income Tax and Enforcement Directorate to check the flow of black money.

This system was originally introduced during the Bihar State elections in 2010 and tried again in the recent polls to five States.

In spite of these measures, the CEO had to admit in May 2011 after the State elections that in spite of all these efforts, "the cancer of money and muscle power could not be wholly checked". The explanation for the huge amount of huge investments into candidates' elections is that Indian politicians are basically professional only in one field—politics. Most of them hold no qualifications for other sources of employment, have no known channels of income either. They have to depend on "unlimited patronage" from powerful business or political blocks.

In the process, a relationship based on quid pro quo naturally develops. Over time, a nexus has become institutionalised between big business and politics.

Therefore big business and politics continue to feed on each other. In 2011, full two decades after the launch of the liberalisation process, we still see every corporate giant knocking on the doors of ministers and bureaucrats. Crony capitalism has become a way of life. What is the way out? Should we simply surrender to greedy politicians and their lackeys? Obviously not. Every political party has got to realise that people have started punishing the corrupt through the ballot.

—16 June, 2011, The Pioneer

The Greatest Mess since Partition

India has consciously integrated its economy, society and politics with the World Capitalist Order and a kind of national political consensus exists among the parties and groups that India should actively participate in all global organisations and institutions to achieve a reasonably high level of rate of economic growth. But though India has achieved a new status of an emerging economy along with China, it continues to accept American pre-eminence in bilateral relationships. The Atal Bihari Vajpayee-led NDA coalition government from 1998 to 2004 and the Manmohan Singh-led UPA government from 2004 to 2011 have made special efforts to remain loyal allies of the US. The Vajpayee government, which had gone out of its way to align with the US, was shocked in 2000 when US President Bill Clinton termed South Asia as the most dangerous place on earth because of the nuclear tests in India and Pakistan in 1998. The Manmohan Singh government also pursued Vajpayee's foreign policy and made every effort, with American support, to sign a nuclear strategic treaty for peaceful purposes in 2008. The Manmohan Singh government relentlessly pursued the Americans to allow nuclear plants for energy needs while forgetting that American multinationals are keen on such a treaty because of the prospective business deals. Manmohan visited America in 2009 to invite Barack Obama, who came with a powerful delegation of multinational corporation heads. France, Russia and other countries were waiting for America to make its move and open up business opportunities for them. America signed the nuclear treaty with India because it was business, because India needed nuclear equipment, technology and plants. Second, it is known that the US economy is facing serious crisis. Paul Krugman, a Nobel Prize winning economist, has warned repeatedly that unemployment in America is growing at an alarming rate and on June 11, 2011, he said, 'America's job drought has gone on so long that the average American has been out of work for almost forty weeks'. Therefore, America needs business opportunities and India is a lucrative business market for American multinationals in the nuclear field. When the US lost the $10.4 billion tender for 126 combat jets in April 2011, US Secretary of State Hillary Clinton and US Ambassador to India Timothy J Roemer expressed their resentment to the Indian Prime Minister. The government of India immediately compensated the Americans when it agreed to buy Boeing C-17s for $4.1 billion. Roemer observed that the sale strengthens strategic ties between the American and the Indian armed forces. He added that the US is committed to sharing expertise and cutting-edge technology with India in a way that has economic benefits for India and the US. This shows that foreign policy is an extension of economic, defence and strategic interests. Our foreign policy makers could have bargained with the Americans if they had realised that America is in an economic crisis and needs India's markets.

America has done nothing for India after Pakistan exported the terrorist attack on Mumbai. Indians were the first to jump the queue in condemning the terrorist attacks on New York on September 11, 2001. India remained quiet when the Americans attacked Saddam Hussein on the pretext of fighting global terrorism in a post-2001 situation. Even now, the foreign policy makers of India are not worried about the implications of NATO presence in Afghanistan. The only beneficiary of the ten-year-old anti-Taliban war in Afghanistan is Pakistan, which has been armed to the teeth by the Americans. Pakistan has no compulsion to sit with India and resolve bilateral disputes because America has financially and militarily equipped Pakistan in its war against Afghanistan. India's pleas to the Americans that a militarised Pakistan is a threat to India has not been responded to positively by the Americans. It clearly shows that India does not carry conviction with the Americans on Pakistan. It is one-way traffic and is a failed foreign policy because India is conscious of American interests and Americans are not reciprocating to India's concerns. Not only this. India has interests in Afghanistan because it is our window to Central Asia. But a militarily well-equipped Pakistan has an upper hand over India on Afghanistan. India has invested in the infrastructural development of a war-devastated Afghanistan, but it is Pakistan, a military ally of America, which has every capacity to checkmate Indian influence in Afghanistan. The American military presence in South Asia has decisively harmed India's national interest in the region. Indians are paying a high cost for following a flawed foreign policy by not giving a clear message to the Americans that the guiding principle has to be bilateral reciprocity and mutuality. It is not only the Americans who are investing in Indian economic growth; Indians like Mukesh Ambani have also invested capital in America. So, is it interdependence or dominance and dependence? The Americans have successfully arm-twisted the Indians on many business and strategic projects but the Indians have failed to convince the Americans that they are following a policy of tilt towards Pakistan. And in the process, the balance of power between these two countries has been disturbed. An American presence in South Asia has limited utility for India. Hillary Clinton and Pranab Mukherjee, India's finance minister, are meeting in July 2011 and it is incumbent on Mukherjee to convey a firm message to the Americans that bilateral economic relations cannot be delinked from the strategic concerns of India about which America has shown very little concern. This is not bilateralism.

—16 June, 2011, The Financial World

Uncertain Politics Ahead

Soft Hindutva may be the easiest option in the road ahead for the Congress as harping too much on secularism may backfire. But Congress leaders are advised not to repeat the mistake of Narasimha Rao, who delinked the party from its Nehruvian roots

The temple judgment must have come as a great and pleasant surprise to the Sangh Parivar because it is a kind of endorsement of its claim that the matters of "faith and belief" cannot be adjudicated upon. The BJP must be in a self-congratulatory mode because it was put into the defensive when its tall political leaders led a mob which destroyed the disputed structure on December 6, 1992. In spite of the Bommai case judgment, the Supreme Court had upheld the dismissal of the BJP State Governments, which had followed, because they had failed to defend secularism which, according to the judges of the highest Court, constituted the "basic structure of the Constitution of the Republic of India".

Further, when elections were held in those States, the BJP was expecting renewed mandates after it had performed "yeoman's job" for the Hindutva cause. But, to its utter shock, the party was defeated in all the States of the Hindi belt. The BJP could not get political mileage or any dividends whatsoever. The so-called "Hindu" voters did not respond favourably in spite of the Sangh Parivar's dubious achievements in furtherance of the Ram cause.

The Sangh and BJP leaders have always justified and legitimised their march to Ayodhya because as "true believers of Hinduism" they felt they just had to install lord Ram at His birthplace. Now we see the High Court unfortunately putting its seal of approval over the claim based on faith and beliefs; as a logical offshoot that Hindu temple of Ram can be built in Ayodhya. The Sangh Parivar's slogan that the Ram temple would be constructed at the same place where it had actually existed before its destruction has been endorsed by Their Lordships, and the Sangh's pride has been restored.

While the BJP is on cloud nine, the Congress is facing the same old dilemma of Hamlet—"to be or not to be." Its old strategy of soft-Hindutva has been defeated before the undistilled Hindutva of the Sangh. The Congress has been caught in the web of its own deceit. It had hoped to balance Hindutva and secularism and failed to learn lessons from its electoral defeats of the 1990s which had its moorings in its reluctance to unambiguously defend the secular values and especially the Nehruvian legacy.

Narasimha Rao had died a tragic figure because he failed to stand up to the forces which had decided to take the law into their hands. Politically, he could not rise against the temple demand. While a section of priests linked to the Sangh has celebrated the High Court judgment and demanded the immediate construction of the Ram temple, the Congress leadership has issued a wishy washy statement. While Ravi Shankar Prasad of the BJP heroically declared after the judgment that "the majority ruled that the location of the makeshift temple is the birthplace of Ram, and this spot cannot be shifted," the Congress' spokesman, Janardhan Dwivedi, said "We all should welcome and respect the judgment."

Unlike the BJP which is in a celebratory mood, the Congress will have to do a lot of explaining because it has got to operationalise Dwivedi's statement about "welcoming" the judgment. Zafarayab Jilani, the Sunni Wakf Board's lawyer, said that the "High Court's formula of one-third land is not acceptable." When prodded further that the judgment should be read in the spirit of reconciliation in the national interest, he angrily responded that "only Muslims are always asked to make compromises in the national interest and for upholding secularism." This Muslim sentiment cannot be ignored by the Congress, which claims to have a "copyright" on secularism.

The political fallout of the High Court judgment is that the Hindu-Muslim divide has further increased and sharpened. Karl Marx had alerted us to the idea of "false consciousness" and this is really applicable to the BJP because the story of conflicts on disputed places of worship has just begun. In spite of the law for the Protection of Places of Worship, any group can attack any place of religious worship on the plea that it "hurts religious sentiments" because it was allegedly built after destroying an earlier place of worship. A country with a long history has witnessed the destruction of religious places of worship by every community, including Hindus.

Can India survive with the baggage of history based on conflicting beliefs and faiths? Every political party has taken resort to opportunistic tactics. While dealing with problems like Ram Janmabhoomi, the emphasis should be on defending the rule of law, irrespective of religious considerations. Otherwise, the law of the jungle will prevail in the country.

Special reference deserves to be made about imaginary constructions of religious identities for political expediency. It should never be forgotten that cultural diversity and pluralism make up the essence of India and the practitioners of Hinduism and Islam are internally divided into multiple sects and communities. Keeping in mind the present controversy, Tulsidas' *Ramcharitmanas* and Valmiki's *Ramayan,* along with many other *Ramayans,* are poetic imaginations.

—22 June, 2011, The Pioneer

Challenges Facing the Congress

The challenge faced by the Congress party is that while it cannot form a government at the Centre on the basis of its own strength in the Lok Sabha, its coalition partners are also its political competitors, even opponents, in different regions of India. This will translate into a difficult situation in the near future when the Lok Sabha elections are held in 2014.

The central issue is the kind of choices the Congress can make while keeping in mind the fragmented and multi-polar political and electoral map of India. The big issue for the Congress lies in states where it has formed coalitions with other parties both for the Lok Sabha and the state assembly elections. The Congress has not evolved any innovative strategies while dealing with its allies in Tamil Nadu, West Bengal and Maharashtra because the DMK, Trinamool Congress and Nationalist Congress party have always dictated terms and conditions to the Congress in return for their participation in a coalition.

Prime Minister Manmohan Singh and Congress party supremo Sonia remained on the receiving end during the whole process of cabinet-making because the three allies not only decided about their nominees in the Union council of ministers, they also arrogated to themselves the power to decide the ministerial portfolios to be allocated to their nominees. A multi-polar political and party system like that of India requires a 'pole' which can bind and knit together coalitional partners and currently India has the Congress and BJP as the 'two poles' of politics.

The Vajpayee-led coalition at the centre (1998-2004) could work smoothly because its regional coalition partners were committed and aggressive anti-Congress political formations. Also, many groups or leaders, including self-proclaimed secularists like George Fernandes or Ram Vilas Paswan or Sharad Pawar or Nitish Kumar have not considered the communal-fascist BJP as being politically untouchable. The Vajpayee government did not face any challenge from its alliance partners even when Gujarat was burning during the post-Godhra riots in 2002 and none of the alliance partners asked for Narendra Modi's head.

If the BJP can win 180 Lok Sabha seats in the 2014 elections, the country will witness a repeat performance of 'local dynastic bosses' doing business with the BJP without any pangs of conscience. The real challenge is faced by the Congress in the era of coalition governments because unlike the BJP it does not have a definite number of political supporters at the regional and sub-regional levels because all major regional parties are involved in political competition with the Congress.

This is the real explanation for the tight-rope act the Congress has to do while dealing with its coalition partners. The Congress looks shaky and vulnerable while dealing with its collation partners because its major allies have been always negotiating with it from a position of strength as a large number of political groups are completely 'de-ideologised' and none of the regional formations are committed to the politics of 'secularism versus communalism'.

The Congress can expand its political support base if it sets its own house in order. First, the Congress has to confront BJP both organisationally and politically in states where politics is polarised between these two main contenders for power. The Congress cannot blame its coalition partners in states like Madhya Pradesh, Gujarat, Chhattisgarh or Jharkhand where it has been ejected by the BJP because even after being defeated the Congress has failed to project its local authentic leaders as alternatives to BJP CMs who have repeatedly won the elections.

Maharashtra Congress is in a bad shape and the party had to replace its own CMs in less than three years. Will Maharashtra go the Karnataka way because the Congress failed to rise to the occasion? Does the Gujarat Congress have a leader who can match a demagogue like Narendra Modi? Second, Sonia Gandhi has to seriously look inward and rethink about her assets and weaknesses as the supreme leader of the Congress. If she is the leader of the party, she has to behave like a leader and perform surgical organisational restructuring of her defunct grassroots party structures.

Sonia has failed to discipline coalition partners of the UPA. On top of that, her party's PM is known to be a nominee and has not been given any authority to act independently on his own. So, even as one aspect of the problem is that its coalition partners have an 'upper hand' at the Centre and the states, the Congress has also failed to evolve an effective collective leadership to properly guide the party. The ground is slipping away from beneath the Grand Old party, and its fortunes cannot be resurrected and revitalised with the present style of politics.

—25 June, 2011, The Economic Times

The Claws of the Lotus Lovers

The Bharatiya Janata Party (BJP), which always claims to be party in the service of people, has been involved in a great internal struggle for power. The latest round involves party president Nitin Gadkari, who has been accused by Gopinath Munde, the former deputy chief minister of Maharastrha, of playing petty politics and undermining the authority of other leaders in the state. This is a serious charge, because, though the divisions and factionalism within the party is a well known fact, the needle of suspicion this time is on the top leader of the party.

Not very long ago, all hell broke loose in the BJP when, in an interview to a news magazine, Sushama Swaraj squarely held Arun Jaitely responsible for the induction of controversial Reddy brothers of Bellary in the BS Yeddyurappa's cabinet of ministers in Karnataka after the BJP's victory in the state Assembly elections of 2008. The Reddy brothers are allegedly engaged in the business of illegal mining activities, and it is suspected that their active political association with the BJP has proved very beneficial for their business activities. Swaraj comes in the picture because she is perceived as patron-in-chief of the Reddy brothers.

The bubble burst because Swaraj wanted to come clean by dissociating herself from such an unholy relationship. This is the explanation being given for Swaraj's public outburst and by shifting the whole responsibility for mess up in Karnataka BJP on Jaitely, she has tried to distance herself from the muddy waters of the BJP politics in Karnataka. The cat was out of the bag when she further elaborated in this public interview that "she was a victim of jealousies within her own party". Swaraj set the cat among the pigeons, and the BJP leaders, like Rajnath Singh and party president Nitin Gadkarai, publicly contradicted Swaraj on the next day by emphasising that "all cabinet appointments in Karnataka were unanimously agreed upon by the central leadership". Gadkari further stated, "Chief Minister Yedyurappa selected his team of ministers in consultation with the party's central leaders. Therefore, there is absolutely no question of any individual or individuals influencing this process in any manner."

It should not be a public concern if the inner party differences are brought out in the open, because it is a normal affair in every party. Further, Swaraj versus Jaitley battle is not the first time the differences in the BJP have come out in the open. Earlier, the differences between Atal Bihari Vajpayee and Lal Krishna Advani were subject of public knowledge during the term of the National Democratic Alliance (NDA) government form 1998 to 2004. Even the ambitions of Murli Manohar Joshi against the powerful position of Advani in the party were well known. Shatrughan Sinha and Yashwant Sinha, like other leaders of the BJP, have always expressed their disagreement with the party high command, because they want to lead the party in Bihar and Jharkhand respectively.

Even the committed supporters of the BJP are hard-pressed to defend open differences of opinion of their leaders, like Swaraj and Jaitely, because the public posture of the BJP has been that it is a highly disciplined party, and for it ideology is supreme and individual ambitious have no place in it, because everyone in the BJP has a supreme cause to promote. The tall claim of the BJP has been that individuals are subordinate, even secondary, and 'ideology' is the sole guiding force, which binds and unites all those who work within the BJP. Further, the BJP leadership had always made tall claims about its moral and political superiority over its rival and competitor the Congress, which is fragmented and has quarrelsome leaders. The BJP claimed that it was 'different' from the Congress, whereas the hallmark of the BJP was ideological and organisational unity and the Congress was only an 'election-winning machine'.

It deserves to be clearly stated that the BJP is just a political arm or shop of the communal-fascist Hindu organisations, led by the Rashtriya Swayamsevak Sangh (RSS). Hence, the Congress is a normal party, and the BJP is its opposite, because it is an integral part of a Hindu joint family, which has inter-related branches, like the Bajrang Dal, the Vishwa Hindu Parishad, the Akhil Bharatiya Vidyarathi Parishad, et al, and all these components of the joint family are controlled and tightly guided by the RSS. The essence of the BJP cannot be understood without demystifying the ideology of the RSS, which is around the doctrine of a Hindu Rashtra: India is a homeland of Hindus, and the believers of other religions, like Islam or Christianity, are 'outsiders'. The idea of the Hindu Rashtra was elaborated by VD Savarkar and the founder of the RSS Dr. K.B. Hedgewar in the 1920s and nurtured and nourished by MS Golwalkar, the second RSS *sarsanghchalak*, who wanted to make India a Hindu homeland.

This ideology of Hindu *rashtravad* is fundamentally opposed to all the basic philosophical premises and postulates of democracy, secularism and pluralism, which are the foundational pillars of the republican constitution of India. It is not without reason that the Vajpayee-led NDA government appointed a Constitutional Review Commission of handpicked individuals to drastically alter the secular ideology of constitution. The BJP is 'a party with a difference', because it does not believe in the secular, democratic philosophy of the constitution, and it is not without reason that Christian churches have been attacked under the protective umbrella of the BJP government in Karnataka. Navin Patnaik, the Chief Minister of Odisha, got rid of the BJP as an ally before the last Assembly election when he saw the 'communal essence' of the BJP when Christian missionaries were attacked by the various outfits of the Sangh *parivar*. All BJP state governments implement the ideological programme of the Hindu *rashtravadis,* and a protective political umbrella is provided by the BJP governments to public functionaries and institutions which are engaged in the Hinduising activities in their states. The Vajpayee government had provided full security to the Naredra Modi government of Gujarat, where minorities were targeted in March-April 2002.

This is one part of the story. The other part of the story is that the BJP is not at all different than other parties, especially the Congress, and its claim of being 'different' is hollow. A few facts may be mentioned to substantiate the argument that like other parties, the BJP is also sucked in the logic of parliamentary electoral politics. First, political parties definitely 'need' finances for their party and political activities, but in India the distinction between genuine 'need' and 'greed' has been blurred. And, the BJP is not an exception to this general rule. Its erstwhile president Bangaru Laxman was caught red-handed in public for accepting illegal money.

The undercurrent of Swaraj's outburst is that her projection as patron-in-chief of illegal mining oligarchs, like the Reddy brothers, somehow is an attempt to tarnish her image as a 'clean leader'. Second, if the money power plays a crucial role during the elections, the BJP is as much guilty as other parties are, because everyone is following the same rules of the electoral game. The BJP-in-government, whether at the Centre or in the states, has been found guilty of misuse and abuse of power for personal and party gains. The BJP government in Madya Pradesh has been censured by the Supreme Court for using public land for purely party purposes. Third, like every other party, especially the Congress, people have no information about the sources of funds for the party. If the Congress is a suspect, the BJP is not a holy cow in this game. The needle of suspicion has been directed against its Karnataka Chief Minister, and the Lokayukta of Karnataka is investigating the serious acts of commission and omission by the Chief Minister. Fourth, all its tall leaders are involved in factional politics, and its factional fight is played in public in the Rajasthan BJP, where former Chief Minister Vasundhara Raje Scindia is fighting for survival. Gadkari had to work very hard to rehabilitate Uma Bharati in the party, because Madhya Pradesh Chief Minster Shivraj Singh Chauhan feels threatened by her re-entry.

Finally, it is 'a party with a difference', because its ideological fellow travellers, like Asseemananadan or Sadhavi Pragya et al, are practitioners of Hindu ideology of terrorist activities against Muslims. At one level, the Sangh Parivar makes its followers religious fundamentalists and terrorists, and, on the other, its leaders fight 'non-ideological' factional battles to promote self-interest at the cost of other competitors. After all, Swaraj and Jaitley are political competitors, and their open criticsim of each other has nothing to do with the interpretation of the ideology of Hindutva. Incidentally, the BJP 'insiders' have fought their factional battles by alleging that Swaraj, Shatrughan Sinha and Yashwant Sinha are non-RSS entrants to the BJP. The purpose of making this distinction between leaders with RSS background and the non-RSS *wallahs* is to show that the RSS affiliation is a prized qualification.

The upshot of the above narrative is that the controversy about Swaraj and Jaitley clearly shows that leaders within the BJP, like its main opponent the Congress, are engaged in a cut-throat competition. The BJP's claim that it is 'a party with a difference' has become a joke, because it is plagued with inner party differences.

—27 June, 2011, The Financial World (Tehlka)

Challenges Facing Indian Democracy

Even though many great philosophers like Plato, Aristotle, Machiavelli, Hobbes, Rousseau, Hegel and Marx drew our attention to the 'first order' question of 'Who Rules Us', the Anglo-American social theorists like John Locke and John Stuart Mill or the founding fathers of American Republican Democracy, particularly after the declaration of American independence in 1776, shifted focus and brought the issue of democratic governance to the centre-stage of public discourse. Following in the footsteps of modern liberal democratic theorists of the western industrialized capitalist countries, Indian analysts too seem to have relegated the fundamental question of Who Rules Us to the background, preferring instead to grapple with the theory and practice of universal adult franchise based representative democracy.

Any comment on this mainstream discourse must first contend with the actual reality of our democracy-based governance. First, over the fifteen Lok Sabha elections, popular participation and voter turnout in every election has remained high and stable, with the voter showing no fatigue or withdrawal symptoms. The state assembly elections of April/May 2011 in Tamil Nadu, Kerala, Pudicherry, Assam and West Bengal witnessed a voter turnout of 70 to 80 per cent as the ruling parties or coalitions in West Bengal, Tamil Nadu and Kerala became victims of voters' fury and anger. The Indian voter has learnt to punish or reward parties, groups and leaders during the elections, indicating that the level of consciousness of the Indian voter has been completely transformed. It can thus be safely stated that fundamental changes in India will take place *only* on the basis of power of rising consciousness of the voter and *not* on the basis of propositions like 'power flows from the barrel of a gun.'

Second, a competitive multiparty system is considered as the bedrock of representative democracy and it is quite clear that India's multipolar political system consists both of all-India/national parties like the Congress, the BJP, and the Communists, and powerful regional and sub-regional parties and groups, all of whom compete for political power. Moreover, the all-India parties, to be successful, have to align with regional parties. Finally, no incumbent party can take voter support for granted, evidenced by the frequency with which voters have punished ruling parties for their arrogance or misgovernance. All this needs to be welcomed.

The less discussed analytical question relates to the manner in which these parties or groups are themselves organized and the social goals which they claim to pursue. Daniel Bell and Francis Fukuyama, among others, claim that democracies have entered the age of 'End of Ideology' and that any reference to ideological beliefs of parties is out-of-date and that the only goal worth pursuing is 'development', captured best by the rate of growth and accumulation of wealth. The Congress, the BJP, as also all the regionalists, whether as part of coalition governments or on the basis of their own single party government in different states, fully subscribe to this worldview, even identifying state governments as 'most developed' or 'developed' or 'backward' only on the basis of their rate of growth in economy. Chandrababu Naidu, leader of the Telugu Desam Party of Andhra Pradesh, has gone further to categorize the states as 'performers' and 'non-performers' or 'doers' and 'non-doers' on the same basis. This is the context in which Indian democracy is to be situated because 'social equality and distribution' have become dirty words for every political formation and capitalist entrepreneurs, middle class professionals and the czars of real estate have become the new role models of society. The rising rate of growth in the economy has sharpened the levels of social inequality and India is witnessing a rural-urban divide, class-caste divide, and enhanced regional imbalances. In this backdrop of inequality and great social disparities, we see the emergence of many Indias which are in serious conflict on the basis of 'left outs' versus 'the beneficiaries'.

Are political parties and leaders at the national or regional levels really worried about the levels of growing social unrest, a consequence of the alarming growth of inequality in society? The answer to this big question is in the negative and can be substantiated by the weak political response to the challenge of inequality. First, it is uncritically assumed that the regional parties and leaders are more aware than the distant all-India national parties to the actual social discontent which prevails at the grassroots levels in their specific region. The fact is that every regional party is following the same path of economic development which has resulted in the growth of social inequality. Their organizational response to reach the mass of people essentially involves projecting the virtues of the 'Leader' and close family members as the sole saviours of the downtrodden. The impact of these leader-based family shops is evident in the way they govern in their region.

Prime Minister Manmohan Singh and his Home Minister, P. Chidambaram have repeatedly proclaimed that the indigenous 'Left wing Extremism is the greatest threat to Indian security.' Clearly, the regional/ national parties which are in power in the affected states—the Jharkhand Mukti Morcha in Jharkhand, the Biju Janata Dal in Orissa or the BJP in Chhattisgarh—too fully support the strong police and paramilitary based response of the central government to the Naxal problem, especially in the backward and neglected areas inhabited by poor tribals. This is just one example where the writ of elected representative governments is enforced by well-equipped and trained paramilitary and police forces of the Indian state and draconian laws are enforced in response to the demands of the people. While not an all-India situation, it does show that even as growing social inequity and deprivation has created 'many Indias', in as many as nine out of 28 states, the ruling parties survive on the basis of armed might and undemocratic laws.

Second, the model of economic growth has also created a fertile ground for the growth of a communal Sangh Parivar, whose governments in various states are following a policy of 'open targeting' of the minority communities and minority cultures. Even as Narendra Modi, Chief Minister of Gujarat, can easily assemble billionaire industrialists like the Tatas, Ambanis and others to showcase and legitimize his government, there is little concern about the poor of India. Evidently, the emerging power of Asia is only keen to project its successful billionaires and millionaires at the global level.

Third, in a country of starvation deaths and malnutrition, aptly described by economist Utsa Patnaik as the 'Republic of Hunger', the Manmohan Singh government has not been castigated by any regional or all India opposition party for delaying the introduction of the Food Security Act in Parliament. Where is the agenda for the poor in a Shining India? Fourth, the democratic Republic of India is fully integrated with global capitalism with the full consent of all parties, all-India and regional. It appears that the only national political consensus is on the path of capitalist development on the basis of complete global integration and free flow of foreign finance capital. Can real democracy ever thrive in a social situation which glorifies its multi-millionaires while giving a short shrift to the deprived strata of society?

It is our firm belief that the marginalization of the pro-poor communists in politics is dangerous for our democracy. What kind of democracy will we have if the voice of the 'Wretched of the Earth' cannot reach the corridors of power? The reference here is not only to the serious electoral setbacks suffered by the communists in the Lok Sabha elections of 2009 or in the state assembly elections of West Bengal in 2011, even the organized working classes and their struggles have become weaker because of caste based and regional fragmentation of the labouring classes in the last two decades. The growing marginalization of the organized communist parties and communist-led all-Indian working classes is a warning signal because the right-wing shift of Indian polity, culture and society is becoming unstoppable in the absence of any countervailing force.

Elections are a necessary but not a sufficient condition to sustain democracy in a society where organized parties have turned their back on the issues of distribution and equality. John Stuart Mill in '*On Liberty*' warned against privileging 'empty liberty and an abstract individual', reminding us that the individual is a real person, and social inequality is palpable. A polity in which unequal distribution of wealth has created 'plutonomies in which small class fractions control increasingly large portions of wealth' cannot but prove extremely dangerous for the future of Indian democracy.

—June 2011-08-02, Seminar 622

Complexity of Indian Electoral Mood

Psephologists in India and elsewhere claim to make predictions about 'how people vote', but they suffer from the same setbacks as meteorologists whose 'forecasts' are considered most unreliable. Indian psephologists, unlike their counterparts in the west, have to find 'shifts' in the mood and preferences of the electorates in a society which is in flux. Hence, the changing context including unpredictable and unforeseeable political episodes or events have to be kept in mind while making any political calculations about the thinking of the voter.

A few facts may be mentioned to substantiate the argument that the 'memory of preceding experiences' including events or happenings on the eve of elections have determined and decided the end-result of elections. First, the April/May 2011 elections to the West Bengal assembly were contested on the basis of electoral polarisation between Mamata Banerjee and the CPI(M)-led Left Front government. The voters of Bengal had forgotten the contribution of Left Front governments from 1977 onwards and they were impacted by serious acts of omission and commission of the Left Front government from 2007 to 2009. Mamata worked very hard for mobilising the disgruntled and angry voters in her favour. The moral of the story is that voters' confidence has to be won by sustained political mobilisation because voters' choice cannot be 'against' and 'in favour' of a party or a leader unless he can 'identify' with one party or the other.

The voters' support has to be 'won over' and it is a great struggle because multiple parties with diverse social constituencies of their own compete against one another. Second, Mamata was perceived by the voter, especially the poor, Dalit, landless and women, as their benefactor. A pro-poor programme or pronouncements or bribes for the voters are not enough to win elections and 'loyalty' of the voter. Every political party has its assured 'constituencies of voters'. Despite that, the communal-fascist BJP could not get more than 20% of votes for the Lok Sabha from so-called Hindus as its project of constructing a monolith Hindu identity has been rejected by a majority of citizens. Mayawati invented a strategy by winning over the support of 'high castes' whom she had earlier castigated, even abused, for being exploiters of the Dalits. Mulayam Singh Yadav of the Samajwadi Party or Lalu Prasad Yadav of the Rashtriya Janata Dal of Bihar or Ram Vilas Paswan, a claimant to the leadership of Dalits, are just some of the political players in a multi-party democracy of these states.

All these three leaders are in the political wilderness because non-Yadav voters who are in a sizeable majority in these two states of north India have rejected them because of their 'betrayal' of voters' trust.

It is not only at the central level, in major states like Uttar Pradesh and Bihar, a coalition of parties is expected to form governments and this is the reason that the mood of voters and shifts in loyalties cannot be easily predicted because the voter's loyalty is also divided among multiple, competing parties. This 'volatility' of the voter is an essential factor to be kept in mind especially in the transitional stage of Indian society. Congress was considered invincible in electoral battles of UP and it had become a fact that the 'road to power at the Centre passed through Lucknow'. The Congress had a powerful social base of coalition of castes and communities. But this social bloc is in shambles and new claimants like Mulayam, Mayawati and Ajit Singh have succeeded in eroding the Congress social base. Hence, the role of Sonia and Rahul Gandhi assumes great importance because they are making every effort to resurrect the party organisation and win back the support of voters.

The Sonia-Rahul leadership failed to win over voters in Bihar as people were satisfied with the Nitish Kumar government's performance. A lesson from Bihar's failure is that without sustained political mobilisation, the opposition cannot change the mood of voters away from the ruling party at a particular time. Hence, Rahul has made UP his main target of mobilisation against the Mayawati government.

First, Rahul openly identified himself with the Dalit cause to give a message that Mayawati was not the only option available to Dalits. He has also taken up the emotive issue of the land acquisition policy of Mayawati's government and has provided a healing touch to the angry farmers of western Uttar Pradesh. The mood of voters in UP is changing in favour of Congress because anger around secular social causes can hurt the vote banks of casteist sectarians like the Bahujan Samaj Party or Mulayam's Samajwadi Party. Thus, such social dialectics of electoral politics dictate that predictions aren't quite easy.

—30 July, 2011, The Economic Times

Identity and Competitive Electoral Politics

Political parties have always claimed that they can never ignore concrete social reality while contesting elections in a democratic competitive political setting. The social context of competitive electoral politics is determined, even conditioned, by the specifics of concrete living situations of human social groups. The perception of political parties is that specific and distinct identities of individuals and groups cannot be ignored because social human groups are always formed around their distinctiveness of identities. Political parties are expected to negotiate with multiple identity-based groups in human society for the purposes of political mobilization not only during the elections, even after the elections, parties have to grapple with the issues concerning identity-based groups.[1] Richard M. Buck, writing about citizens maintains that '... the full expression of their identity requires meaningful membership in a group...' whose members share their ideas and commitments, ... "[2]

Buck further maintains that identity-based groups become "powerful political force" because they act as "Interest group" and articulate their specific group demands in public. Identity-based groups theorists are defending and legitimizing identity on the basis of an argument, that in a society of multiple, plural and diverse groups, special interests of special groups have to be protected and promoted by sensitizing the public policy makers about the diverse felt needs of identity groups like Religious Minority groups. Equal rights for all citizens can be the proclaimed goal of every democratic political country but equality for all is an abstraction and it has to be concretized only by protecting special and specific rights of religious minorities or caste-based or multiple linguistic groups. The essential argument of the defenders of specific and special rights for numerous identity-based groups is that human society is not an abstraction, on the contrary, it is an association of associations whether based on primordialism or by any other marker including marker by Birth. Hence public policy makers in democracy are under an obligation to promote the well-being of multiple identity-groups and it is the job of political parties to mobilize different identity-based groups for their political empowerment. Electoral politics is competitive and different political parties identify and mobilize different identity groups and its consequence is that parties compete for winning over the support of some identity groups by making them conscious of their distinct identity group rights. Political parties try to win over Muslim minority groups and in the process of political competition, another political party tries to identity itself with Sikh or Christian minority groups. This logic of competitive politics is inherently divisive because different parties compete for winning over the loyalty of different, generally, opposite identity-based groups like Muslims or Sikhs or Christian *et al.*

The moot question is: are the champions of rights for special and separate identity groups able to promote 'equality' among groups in democratic society? Identity groups contest for special rights to make the abstract idea of equality as really meaningful and substantive. Political parties fight for special rights for identity-based groups on the agenda of promoting equal participation of especially minority groups in the political system and these champions of special rights of identity-based groups may have laudable goal of the deepening of social equality in society but forget that they may be, in the final analysis, creating 'inequality' within their own groups because the logic of process of distribution of benefits even among groups is that the 'elite' of the group are able to corner more benefits than those who are at the bottom of the ladder. After all identity-based groups are also hierarchical and internally differentiated and their clamour for 'equality; in society can end up in creating 'inequality' within their own groups Richard M. Buck observers:

"But this structural benefit of identity groups is not without its drawbacks. Because identity groups are concerned primarily with the interests of the group, one can foresee a tendency of these groups to favour these group interests over individual interests of other citizens, as well as the citizens of their own groups. Put otherwise, the total perspective of identity groups may direct them to act in ways that clearly compromise the individual liberties of citizens outside of (and, perhaps, within) their own group. Such an outlook is inconsistent with the core ideas of democracy...."[3]

Need for an Alternative Politics

Generally political parties and groups with limited social goals are always in search of Identity versus Identity political mobilizational social constituencies because identification of a party with specific. Identity group provides that party an assured though limited social base. A section of Indian scholars maintain that caste identity is a social reality, its logic is appropriated by political parties which operate on the basis of caste versus caste and sub-caste versus sub-caste politics. Caste-based parties become a reality because if caste in India is a reality, parties cannot ignore caste-based mobilization in politics. The alternative to identity politics is an agenda of mobilization of large social solidarities which can transcend fragmented identity based parties. If identity groups are promoters of specific 'interests' of specific identity groups, politics of large scale social transformation is the legitimate agenda of national parties and this political platform of social transformation can create an alternative social constituency which acts as collectivity of fragmented identity groups. Social equality cannot be a goal of fragmented identity groups. An equal society is inclusive of all underclasses and underprivileged and exploited groups which are united and mobilized on the goal of equality for all irrespective of identities based on birth or religion or caste or race or ethnicity. This fact has been validated by the history of modern industrial capitalist societies that separate, fragmented identity groups cannot achieve the goal of social equality and liberty for the whole society. If the dominant ideology of capitalism and the laws of capitalist development lead to the creation of unequal structures of social relations, the quest for equality for minority groups is bound to end in a failure because if whole society is based on the fundamental principle of 'inequality', it cannot provide equality to social identity based fragmented. Identity groups are part of a social whole but the whole society is not a sum-total of separate parts and elements. This led French philosopher Foucault to take a stand on the problematic of 'Identity' and he maintains that '....Understanding or not understanding, others identities can result in appreciation or denigration, accommodation or separation, assimilation or extermination. Together, the formations, functions and effects of identity can draw physical boundaries between peoples,...[4]

The sum um and substance of above argument is identity-based political mobilization is not at all inevitable in political electoral democracy, on the contrary, an alternative ideological mobilization by political parties can also win elections in which large social solidarity blocs are mobilized around the goal of establishing an equal society. Human beings can transcend their narrow identity-based markers and create united platforms if political parties mobilize voters on the basis of transformational programmatic politics. It is an illusion that groups, whether based on religion or caste or language or race or ethnicity, can promote the cause of their specific identity groups in a society which is essentially based on the foundational principle of inequality and social disparities. Historical evidence cannot be wished away. Multiple identity groups cannot achieve equality for their distinct groups in a society of unequals.

Notes

1. Amy Gautamann, *Identity in Democracy*, Princeton, NJ Princeton University Press, 2003.
2. Richard M. Buck, 'Religion, Identity, and Political Legitimacy: Toward Democratic Inclusion', *Journal of Social Philosophy*, Vol. 39, No. 3, Fall 2008, p. 346.
3. Richard M. Buck, *op. cit.*, 349.
4. James Der Derian, 'Critical encounters in International Relations', *International Social Science Journal,* Paris, March 2008, No. 191, p. 72.

No Socialism in the Preamble? It Means Abandoning Ideals of Equality

The ideology of neo-liberal free-market capitalism has completely vitiated and distorted the thinking of Indians who are not ready to tolerate any reference to the idea of socialism in the Preamble of the Indian Constitution. It is also quite surprising that while dismissing the PIL filed by an NGO against the inclusion of the ideal of socialism based on the 42nd amendment of the Constitution, the honourable judges observed that "this question is highly academic. Let us not go into it now." If the goal of social equality, which is the quintessence of socialism, is an academic issue, it means that Indian society should abandon the national goal of establishing an equal and just social order. It deserves to be clearly mentioned that the root cause of our deep social crisis and social divisions is that Indians have abandoned the national project of building an egalitarian socialist society, abandoned the goal of 'development for all'.

Modern historical experience clearly shows that human beings have been involved in struggles around goals of equality. Every society had to find solutions for dealing with serious discontent. The idea of a welfare state and social market economy guided the policies of many European capitalist countries with a view to heal the wounds created by un-equal growth of wealth under capitalism. The moral of this story of 20th century welfare capitalism is that the extension of the system of universal adult franchise-based democracy necessitated state intervention for the fulfilment of basic needs of every group in society before profit-making capitalists could pursue their economic goals.

Capitalism and democracy develop an antagonistic relationship and this contradiction can be resolved only by linking socialism with democracy. Nehru's consensus-based politics was solidly grounded on the foundations of a national project of democracy, secularism and socialism. The present deep-rooted crisis in India is the result of the ongoing process of individual profit-seeking that has replaced the idea of a social collective based on the project of sharing of the fruits of development. This is possible only under socialism.

Politics Beyond Parties

The socially felt needs of multiple, diverse groups in a pluralist, democratic system are articulated by organised political parties, which contest for control over the levers of governmental power for providing public goods and services. While political parties play a pre-eminent role in the functioning of a democratic political system, they do not exhaust the whole social space and many voluntary social groups make efforts to bring to the notice of decision-makers crucial issues and concerns of different special groups.

India has many organised, specialised groups like business associations, trade unions and formal bodies of professional groups like the bar councils, which play an active role in the articulation of special demands of groups that need to be addressed by the government. In the process, these voluntary, social groups broaden the agenda of governance by complementing and supplementing the agendas of political parties.

This is only one part of the story because it does not exhaust the whole picture of the living reality of social beings in a society that is witnessing a phase of grand transition. Many strata of Indian society feel completely alienated and disenchanted with the democratic political system and from every mainstream political party because of a feeling that parties have completely abandoned the agenda of inclusive social transformation. An important group of CPI (Maoists) has mobilised the neglected tribal population against the way political parties have functioned in the process of governance. It is instructive, even educative, to understand the phenomenon of the growth of the Maoist movement that is fighting the BJP-led government of Chhattisgarh and Madhya Pradesh, regional parties-led governments of Bihar, Jharkhand and Orissa, the Communist-parties-led government of West Bengal and the Congress-led governments of Andhra Pradesh and Maharashtra.

The state of Jharkhand was created with great fanfare as a tribal homeland, and in this state, 19 out of 24 districts are under the control of Maoists who are challenging the authority of the Indian state. The prime minister and home minister have repeatedly maintained that left-wing extremism is the greatest threat to the Indian democratic state and central and state governments have decided to meet their challenge head on. Incidentally, one lakh cases filed against the tribals in Jharkhand were withdrawn at the behest of the Union government because the tribals were being prosecuted for trivial violations of law.

It is not only harassment and humiliation at the hands of government functionaries that the poor tribals and Dalits have to put up with but local contractors and land grabbers also humiliate them. The 'trickle down' benefits from economic development have not reached the poor and so the Maoists are able to mobilise dissatisfied, deprived tribals against the model of economic development pursued by mainstream parties during the past 60 years since Independence. The mainstream parties are opposed by the Maoists because of a conviction that these parties have failed to implement socially transformative agenda. In fact, one-third of the country has been left behind because of the path of development followed by the existing parties.

If the extreme Left is challenging the political system for its Himalayan failure to achieve any positive good, the extreme Right represented by the Sangh Parivar is struggling to capture state power with a view to subvert the system based on emotive appeals around Hindu religious symbols like Ram Janmabhoomi or its latest gimmickry of Gau Gram Yatra in the villages. The RSS has called it the 'biggest mass mobilisation project since the Ram Janmabhoomi movement.'

If the extreme Maoists movement is sustained by the deprived, disenchanted tribals, the RSS and the Parivar are indoctrinating the alienated, half-educated, unemployed or underemployed youth for the establishment of a Hindu Rashtra instead of a secular state. European history teaches us that fascism, Nazism and racially engineered hate campaigns were based on ideology but the carriers of this ideology were the youth of Germany and Italy who were the worst victims of economic depression and crisis. After all, Raj Thackerey, leader of fascist Maharasthra Navnirman Sena can bring the financial capital of India to a halt with the support of lumpen youth who are made to target 'the outsider' in Mumbai.

Mainstream political parties have to wake up because Indian democracy is facing a fundamental challenge from the extreme Left and extreme Right and in this polarisation, the defenders of democratic social transformation of India will be the losers. The moot question is: why have the Maoists received the support and acceptability of the tribals? What is the explanation for the emergence of this movement from the social soil of India? It does not require a magician to state that the tribals of India are the victims of rampant corruption and mis-governance. Similarly, why has the RSS, a completely anti-system movement, grown in strength? The answer is political parties have been reduced to the level of election winning machines without any large vision of India.

—*Economic Times*

Spreading Canards in the Name of Fighting Corruption

The public discourse on corruption in public life has come to occupy a central space in India. The context is important because continuing exposures of cases of corruption against tallest political leaders, high level of bureaucrats and multi-billionaire businessmen of the country have shaken the faith of an average Indian in the system of governance.

A question, however, has been agitating the minds of ordinary Indians about the powerful nexus which exists among politicians, bureaucrats and industrial class who are collectively involved in illegal transactions by bending laws and procedures of Government. Every powerful group — democratically-elected politicians, professional bureaucrats and entrepreneurs — has become 'suspect' in the eye of law-abiding citizens. A feeling has developed that laws of the country are meant only for the poor and helpless masses.

A democratic system of governance cannot survive or, for that matter, thrive if people are conditioned in believing that every 'elected representative' is corrupt and misuses his power to appropriate public resources and finances for private personal and family purposes. This milieu of negativism, cynicism and complete distrust in constitutionally-established institutions for governance can become a fertile ground for the birth of anti-democratic adventurists. Historical evidence clearly shows that democracy can be subverted and sabotaged by anti-democratic military Generals or fascist and Nazis like Hitler of Germany or Mussolini of Italy or General Franco of Spain or near home General Ayub Khan of Pakistan if the 'public mood' turns against electoral process which is projected as villain of the piece because democracy is labeled as a breeding ground for corruption.

Therefore, Indians should be worried about the ongoing high velocity campaign against corruption in democracy because a message is spread that institutional arrangement of checks and balances provided in the Indian Constitution has completely become dysfunctional and has failed to punish the guilty and corrupt. A few facts may be mentioned to substantiate the argument that the ongoing campaign that every elected political representative is 'corrupt' and elections are won only with a purpose to exercise control over public resources for self-advancement could pose a threat to all the institutions of parliamentary system established by the Constitution of India.

Anna Hazare is leading an anti-corruption movement that has a fascist overtone because even Parliament, which represents political diversity of India, is being commanded to accept the so-called Jan Lokpal Bill drafted by Team Anna. Parliament is the pillar of Indian democracy and every Bill gets democratic approval or rejection on the floor of both the Houses of Parliament.

Team Anna during its meeting with Parliamentary Standing Committee which is seized of the Lokpal Bill has asked for rejection of the Bill under consideration of Parliament and 'accept' the Bill prepared by the group. The demand to 'accept' their Bill or 'face' public anger which is manipulated by undertaking emotive steps like 'fast-unto-death' is not justifiable.

It is bizarre, to say the least, that Anna Hazare is adopting coercive methods to achieve his goal. He is challenging the constitutional and legal rights of elected representatives to perform their legitimate functions. The mood of the people is that the Supreme Court and the High Courts are interfering, without any opposition from any crusader of corruption, in the legitimate areas of the functioning of the executive.

Judiciary has decided to launch investigations under its own supervision against suspect corrupt politicians or bureaucrats or captains of industry. Judiciary has served a vote of no-confidence against investigating agencies of the Government which are legally accountable only to the elected Council of Ministers, whether at the Centre or in States.

The honourable judges have not hesitated to directly perform the duties of political executive on the plea that politicians cannot be trusted to launch proper investigations against cases of alleged corruption in public life.

It should not be at all surprising to find judges performing roles which they are not meant to undertake because anti-corruption crusaders have created an atmosphere against politics per se where everyone, including judges, are enjoying a new status of 'cleansing' the country of corruption. Not to be best behind the Deputy Comptroller and Auditor General decided to call a Press conference to release report on corruption.

Media — both print and audio-visual — is a pillar of democracy and in every democracy it acts as a watchdog of public interest, concerns and issues. The media in India, especially, the audio-visual, is enjoying its new power because under the present circumstances, all self-imposed and self-denying limitations get excused because people are interested in stories about corruption in public life. This is the reason that Baba Ramdev and Anna Hazare have settled down in the capital of India to launch their tirade against democratic politics because audio-visual media advertises their rhetoric every day.

Even ordinary law and order maintenance forces are often under pressure of judicial or media scrutiny, while dealing with crowd agitating for a sacred and holy cause against corruption in public life. Can democratic governance of any kind function when judiciary, media, Comptroller and Auditor-General, agitators are setting the agenda for political executive, parliament and the apparatus of the state?

The so-called anti-corruption sentiment has become so dominant that every democratic institution of governance is under cloud of widespread suspicion.

—22, August, 2011, The Pioneer

Potential of Mass Movements

Anna Hazare's agitation in defence of his version of the Lokpal Bill seems to have revived public memories of the 1974-75 Jayaprakash Narayan-led anti-corruption mass agitation, especially among the new generation of technology-driven middle class youth in metropolitan towns of India. But can Anna Hazare's anti-corruption crusade become a benchmark comparable with the historical mass mobilisation movements launched by Gandhi from 1920 to 1947 or the one popularly known as the JP movement of 1974-75? A mass movement has to be distinguished from political mobilisation undertaken by every political party in a competitive democracy because, unlike parties which mobilise their voters and supporters for winning an election, people's movements are launched for cleansing the system of its fundamental ills. Gandhi prepared Indians to fight the struggle for Independence and for this mass struggle he created a united social bloc of castes, classes, religions, regions and women. The Gandhian movement was socially broad-based and inclusive of all major group identities of the country. The JP movement, unlike Gandhi's struggles, had a limited reach, where he raised anti-corruption issues facing India.

Further, JP, unlike Gandhi, had no mass base of his own, and he led the movement on the basis of cadre provided by Lohia socialists, the Rashtriya Swayamsevak Sangh (RSS) and the Jan Sangh. Essentially, JP launched a movement on the corruption issue primarily directed against Indira Gandhi as an individual and as a leader of a corrupt party and government.

The lesson from the JP movement is that a large-scale mass movement has to be a product of preceding small-scale mobilisations as Gandhi did from the 1920s to 1947. Anna Hazare's movement has some salient features that are a replication of the JP movement, but it has nothing in common with Gandhian movements. Hazare's movement has spread in towns and cities, especially after his arrest by Delhi Police on August 16 and angry people have come out on the road in support of him. It is a repeat story, because the JP movement had assumed an all-India status only when the

Allahabad High Court judgment of June 1975 set aside the election of Prime Minister Indira Gandhi.

This support of the urban middle and lower middle class to Hazare is not only because of his anti-corruption crusade but because it is also an expression of their general frustration with the existing situation for which the easy whipping boy is the Manmohan Singh government. Further, Hazare himself and many of his supporters on the streets are targeting corrupt politicians, but in reality they are themselves apolitical, even anti-politics, in their daily life and ideological value system. Hazare has debunked the system of elections by publicly stating that 'elections are won by bribing the voter' and his complete lack of faith in the democratic process of India can be summed up in his oft-repeated statement that 'the transfer of power after 1947 was from the 'white' to the 'brown' and 'black' Indians and 'nothing has changed during the last 64 years of India's Independence'.

Further, unlike Gandhi, Hazare who has no faith in democracy, has adopted 'fascistic methods' to get a seal of approval by Parliament for his demand. This has nothing to do with Gandhian movements because Gandhi suspended his movements and never feared to negotiate with the colonial rulers. Anna, like JP, has been compelled to depend on the mobilisation machine of the Sangh Parivar and its communal-fascist cadre of the RSS. The BJP within Parliament and the whole joint family of the Sangh Parivar on the streets are providing the whole structure of support to keep the pot boiling to stigmatise the Congress, its main rival in politics.

Gandhi's movements had a long-term impact on Indian public life, Hazare's movement, like the JP movement, has political consequences and its impact will be felt only in electoral politics. The age of large-scale united all-India mass movements has come to an end because a socially and regionally fragmented country will have, and has been, witnessing local/regional movements or caste-based movements. Our national identity, which was created by Gandhian struggles from Kohima to Peshawar, has been pushed to the background by movements launched by 'fragments' on particularist demands of sections of society. Political competition among parties around 'local grievances' has become the reality of democratic India. It is no one's case that 'politics' will be missing from social movements; the only issue, as raised by the German philosopher Habermas, is that every social movement should be critically evaluated on the basis of its leadership, its social base, and the social cause pursued by the leaders. On the basis of the analytical yardstick suggested by Habermas, Hazare's movement and the social support generated by it clearly reveals that the communal-fascist Sangh Parivar is the main driver of this movement.

—24 August, 2011, Economic Times,

Section II
Foreign Policy

Soft PM's Soft Stand on Terror

Our Ambassadors and High Commissioners who gathered in Delhi for their annual conference have returned without being told what steps are being taken by Government to counter Pakistani perfidy

The recently-held annual conference of 112 heads of missions abroad provided the perfect platform for India to acquaint other countries about the challenges being faced by the country from across its borders. But India failed to put across the point.

On the first day, while addressing the conference, Minister of External Affairs SM Krishna conveyed a clear message to all diplomats that terrorism was India's most important foreign and national security concern and the threat of terrorism faced by India should be highlighted. The message was reiterated by Prime Minister Manmohan Singh on August 25 as well.

"India has been a victim of terrorism and it was essential that global terrorism is tackled with full vigour," Mr Singh said.

So far, so good.

But shockingly the Prime Minister did not identify the source of terrorist threat to India. We are not facing an abstract or imaginary enemy because the Taliban and jihadis are not indulging in terrorist activities against India from an unidentifiable country. We know that terrorist activities are emanating from Pakistan.

The heads of missions had not gathered in New Delhi to listen to bland statements on terrorism being threat to India's security. It was expected of the Prime Minister to elaborate the UPA Government's foreign policy towards Pakistan, apart from spelling out its expectations from the neighbouring country.

The pernicious role of the Taliban in waging a war against India should have been mentioned so that the heads of missions drive home the point with details and facts about the ground situation and build international pressure to make Pakistan see reason on the issue of terrorist threat to India.

During the five-day conclave, the Prime Minister said that "India has a stake in the prosperity and stability of all our South Asian neighbours. We should strive to engage our neighbours constructively and resolve differences through peaceful means and negotiations."

This policy approach of the Prime Minister on South Asia is absolutely appropriate and there is a need for full 'engagement' with all our South Asian neighbouring countries. But Mr Singh forgot to mention that the country is facing a lot of difficulties and uncertainties in bilateral and multilateral relationship in the South Asia region. For instance, a disturbed Afghanistan can be of adverse implications on India's security and national interests.

It is deplorable that Indian diplomats were not conveyed any message by the Prime Minister on the ongoing internal war in Afghanistan and its impact on India's relations with Pakistan and Afghanistan. Does India approve of US's policy of military intervention in Afghanistan or it is going to be another Waterloo for America? Any political upheaval in Afghanistan has consequences for India via Pakistan and any success of the Taliban in Afghanistan will create serious problems for India's security via Pakistan.

Mr Singh indulged in platitudes while stating that "economics determines foreign policy agendas in this age of globalisation". Appallingly, he forgot to mention that along with economic agenda of foreign policy, Indian diplomats have to engage themselves at global level about the terror threats faced by India. The agenda of global cooperation does not hang in the air, it has to be based on the concrete economic and strategic needs of the country, but unfortunately the Prime Minister completely failed to concretise the required linkages between India's priorities and global agenda.

Mr Singh rightly said that national "insularity was not an option," but he ducked the issue of relating India's domestic requirements and the nature of linkages which India should have with multiple centres of power.

Polarisation of political opinion on the India-US civilian nuclear deal and the surrender at Sharm el-Sheikh failed to teach the UPA Government any lesson. Hence it is for the Government to engage with the Opposition parties and evolve a national consensus on foreign policy and present it before its diplomats and foreign policy messengers.

This weakness on the foreign policy front acts as a handicap for Indian diplomats who have to articulate in very concrete terms foreign policy issues. The five-day conclave was indeed a waste of time, energy and resources.

—2 September, 2009, The Pioneer

Ad-Hocism as Foreign Policy

It is hardly expected of our regional political party leaders to offer an appropriate and coherent agenda of foreign and security policies for the country because their worldview is limited—even narrowly confined—to a universe of reality which is co-terminus with their own State or region or even sub-region. However, a national party in power at the Centre, with a coalition of other parties, cannot be forgiven if it fails to do so.

First, by de-hyphenating terrorism and referring to the Baluchistan issue in a joint communique issued after the meeting between Indian and Pakistani Prime Ministers at Sharm el-Sheikh in July, the Manmohan Singh Government has completely disregarded the public opinion back home. The UPA Government's 'ad-hocism' was further demonstrated on the issue of intrusions by the Chinese in the Indian territory. The issue of Chinese intrusion continued to engage the attention of Indians, including a section of former diplomats and military personnel. But the Government did not consider it proper to state facts and it completely failed to provide effective leadership on such a sensitive issue.

When the Manmohan Singh Government finally woke up, the Government in its wisdom warned the media to stop the 'China hype' because it could be 'dangerous' to the bilateral relations of the two countries. What a response by a Government of a democratic country?

The problem of ill-defined boundaries between India and China is root to the ups and downs in relationship. All kind of conflicting statements were made by all and sundry and the Government repeatedly stated that India-China relations are quite 'normal'. Instead, the focus was on scientist K Santhanam's statement that Pokharan II nuclear test of 1998 was a 'dud'. The Government should have either firmly snubbed him or it should have maintained that the statements in defence of the effectiveness of nuclear test made by former President Abdul Kalam and former NSA Brajesh Mishra are authentic and the Government does not accept any other version on this issue. Later, National Security Advisor MK Narayanan made an official statement that India does not need any more nuclear tests because Pokharan II of 1998 was quite adequate.

Why Such Silences on Sensitive Issues of Foreign and Security Policies?

To top it all, former Pakistani President Pervez Musharraf's statement that Pakistan had always used American aid to build its security apparatus against India, spoiled the UPA Government's party of completing 100 days in office. Should not have the Government lobbied against Gen Musharraf's claim and ask the US to reconsider its monetary help to Pakistan in its fight against terrorism? But no. And that US as a friend has been the latest discovery of the Manmohan Singh Government. In the inimitable words of VK Krishna Menon, American guns supplied to Pakistan cannot fire only in one direction because every gun can be turned against an enemy by the person who possesses that gun.

The US has been equipping Pakistan for fight against Taliban, Al Qaeda and in the ongoing American-led war in Afghanistan. Does the UPA Government accept this alibi of America and Pakistan and still continue to believe Americans or Pakistanis?

Pakistan has its own interests in Afghanistan and those interests do not converge with the national interests of Americans in this whole region of south and central Asia. India also has its own interests in Afghanistan but in this ongoing war of America in Afghanistan, it is not India but Pakistan which carries great leverage with the Americans. This deep linkage between America and Pakistan has been revealed in a report on September 22 by the US General Stanley McChrystal in which he has warned that Indian influence in Afghanistan has been increasing and he further states that "... increasing Indian influence in Afghanistan is likely to exacerbate regional tensions and encourage Pakistani countermeasures in Afghanistan or India".

This report by an American General again exposes the lack of foresight in Indian policymaking because Afghani people or the Hamid Karzai Government may be positive about India's economic and humanitarian activities in the building of Afghanistan but we do not have any military leverage to defend our interests in Afghanistan. On the other hand, Pakistan, Al Qaeda and Taliban forces are determined to rule over Afghanistan where Indians will have no role to play.

It should not be forgotten that several workers from India and even the Indian Embassy have been targeted by Islamists in Afghanistan who enjoy patronage and protection of Pakistan.

—28 September, 2009, The Pioneer

Gungi Gudiya who Took on Uncle Sam

Indira Gandhi was essentially a democrat and though her critics pillory her over the Emergency, nobody can deny that her outlook was defined by the urge to include the poorest in India's growth story

The social dialectics of a democracy are quite complex and contradictory. How could Indira Gandhi, a 'puppet' of the Congress party bosses become the Amaa of the poor, the Dalits and the women of rural India? How could she return to power on the basis of votes of the same voters who had rejected, even punished her in the Lok Sabha election of 1977? How could she win two-third of the seats in 1971 and 1979? How could she become the 'sole face' of the Congress and its 'sole successful campaigner'? How could she reduce, electorally, the Opposition parties to the position of great insignificance? How could she carry the verdict of voters on her shoulders in spite of the opposition and the sabotaging politicking of fellow Congressmen? Indira was a messiah of the poor and her promises carried great credibility and conviction with the oppressed. Her Garibi Hatao programme evoked enthusiastic endorsement from the masses. Bank nationalisation opened the doors for the Dalits who got jobs in modern organisations.

The Congress had opted for Indira in 1966 on the basis of a premise that as Nehru's daughter she would win elections for the party and as Prime Minister she would toe the line set by the bigwigs. They were not motivated by any sense of loyalty to her. In 1966, she was brought in as an interim Prime Minister after Lal Bahadur Shastri's death. The electoral reverses suffered by the Congress in 1967 brought into the open the conflicts among the various contenders for the prime ministership.

Indira's sense of political insecurity and anxiety forever haunted her and this was revealed when she 'split' the Congress in 1969 and asked for early polls in 1971. She got a confidence boost when that election resulted in a two-thirds majority for the Congress. For a few years, the nation saw a new Indira Gandhi bringing to an end the hesitant Indira of 1966-1971. She showed this new self-confidence while dealing with the crisis of Bangladesh.

During this period, the entire top brass of the party was reduced to the status of a cipher and the Congress had only one boss, i.e. Indira herself. Authority in the party, in the ultimate analysis, got concentrated in Indira's hands. This supreme trait was not confined to the affairs of the Congress; the affairs of the government were also conducted by her on the basis of the 'buck stops here' principle.

The only purpose behind the declaration of the Emergency in 1975 was to protect and defend Indira, the Prime Minister, who was under political siege. Power flowed from the Constitution till it protected Indira in power and the Constitution was expendable when it proved inconvenient to her. It clearly shows that Indira's authoritarian tendencies were integral to her philosophy of governance. This manifested itself in the Emergency and while dealing with 'movements' like the Assam student's demands.

In her obsession with the Opposition, she often adopted Machiavellian methods. To counter the Akalis, she created a Frankenstein in Jarnail Singh Bhindranwalla. To her, the end justified the means. She also created politics of the personality-cult when the need of the hour was to work with constitutionally provided institutions. This face of Indira should not be forgotten by future generations—they should look out for leaders like her who ride rough shod over Constitutional institutions for governance.

When the history of Indira's 15 years in power is written, there may emerge a ruthless leader who was also the darling of the poor.

Historical judgments are ruthless. But it is impossible for contemporary intelligentsia to objectively evaluate her legacy. Indian nationalists cannot forget her contribution to nation building, especially the events leading to the emergence of Bangladesh, especially the rebuff she gave to Richard Nixon and Henry Kissinger.

She also saved India's nascent economy. For today's great liberalisers it is impossible to comprehend the delicate condition that India was in the 1960s under pressure from global capitalism. The victims of the Emergency of 1975-77 cannot accept anything good to be written about Indira. This was Indira, who dominated the political scene and history from 1966 to 1984. She cannot be ignored either by contemporaries or posterity.

What is the real legacy of Indira? First, Indira loved India and was a zealous defender of her sovereignty. Her dialectical relationship with India spelt that love for India was equal to love for ruthless exercise of personal power for the defense of national interest, which got intertwined with her own. Second, Indira taught Indians that democracy can be subverted by a Prime Minster unless Opposition parties are vigilant. Third, only Indians can defend their own freedom from hostile powerful countries and no one will stand for India if the country is facing domestic or external problems.

—31 October, 2009, The Pioneer

A Shared Destiny: India, China can Rise by Working Together

Prime Minister Manmohan Singh and his Chinese counterpart Wen Jiabao held a bilateral meeting on October 24 during a Summit of the Association of South East Asian Nations. It was followed by External Affairs Minister SM Krishna meeting with his counterpart Yang Jiechi on October 27 during a trilateral meeting of India, Russia and China. These two high-powered meetings clearly suggest that both Beijing and New Delhi are keen to continue their dialogue on bilateral issues.

The Chinese and the Indians have to appreciate the logic of the 21st century which has brought great powers along with great responsibilities for the twin emerging economies of Asia. Hence, the terms of 'engagement' between India and China should be dictated by the logic of the present century which the Chinese have characterised as the Asian century. We no more live in a struggling, decolonised Asia of the post-World War II era. Thus, expecting an 'economic miracle' which will lead to a shift in the centre of global power from North America and Europe to Asia will be naive. Within Asia the catalysts for such an 'economic miracle' are India, China, Japan and the East Asian countries. This is the reason why both New Delhi and Beijing are attaching great importance to the idea of ASEAN and an attempt is on to establish a political group, may be an Asian Union or an Asian Common Market, along the lines of the European Union.

Policy-makers cannot ignore macro or mega trends at the international and regional levels because foreign and domestic policies have to respond to the new emerging global challenges. It is essential to keep in mind this framework of the 21st century for understanding the reality of India-China bilateral relations.

Besides, the recent bilateral meetings between New Delhi and Beijing assume significance in the wake of the discord that had arisen between the two neighbours over the border issue. Despite serious differences of opinion on the demarcation of the border, Prime Minister Manmohan Singh at the ASEAN summit said that India will have a "functional cooperation" with China. The two have long coordinated approach on climate change and are actively cooperating in negotiations on global trade at the World Trade Organization. The two have also dramatically expanded their bilateral trade relations: In 2005 India and China signed the Strategic and Cooperative Partnership for Peace and Prosperity pact and, in 2008, Prime Minster Manmohan Singh and Chinese President Hu Jintao brought out a Shared Vision Document.

This engagement between India and China is for mutual benefit. The growing partnership between the two countries is the result of the logic of the 21st century.

This does not mean that India and China do not have areas of mutual conflict that have created tension between them. While the border dispute is a historical legacy, the construction of a dam across the Brahmaputra by China without taking India into confidence, and its involvement with projects in Pakistan-occupied Kashmir have naturally generated ill-feelings about Beijing in New Delhi.

With the Indian and Chinese Prime Ministers agreeing last month to gradually narrow differences on border issues, the focal point of the bilateral relationship is bound to shift. It will all boil down to whether China recognises the special status that India occupies in Asia and does India reciprocate the same feeling for the Chinese.

Besides, China must realise that its relationship with Pakistan will not lead it anywhere as the latter is facing a number of serious internal crises. Therefore, China's Pakistan card, suspected to be a counter-India strategy, is fast losing its significance. At the end of the day, the dialogue between these two neighbouring giants will sometimes be conducted in friendly and sometimes in not so friendly conditions. But there is no denying that dialogue is the only way forward to find solutions to the various bilateral issues.

—3 November, 2009, The Pioneer

India-China: Cold Peace

The Cold War and a bipolar global system ended in 1989 with the fall of the Berlin Wall and the liquidation of the erstwhile Soviet Union in 1991. The former Cold War system of international relations, however, has been replaced by a system of Cold Peace between competing powerful countries such as India and China or the US and China. The salient feature of the era of Cold Peace between powerful countries like India and China is that both have conflicting and competing areas of interest and, at the same time, both have clearly opted for a path of friendly or formal methods of resolving their bilateral disputes.

If Indians got disturbing news about the proposed construction of a dam on the Brahmaputra by the Chinese a few weeks ago, Prime Minister Manmohan Singh and his Chinese counterpart Wen Jiabao held a bilateral meeting in Thailand on October 25 during an ASEAN Summit. The Indian PM declared at the summit that despite serious differences of opinion on the demarcation of the border and other contentious bilateral disputes, India will have 'functional cooperation' with China.

Dr Singh has spelt out the nuances of India's approach towards China by stating during the summit that he agreed with premier Wen that "existing mechanisms for bilateral cooperation should be used to resolve all issues amicably". The process of continuing the dialogue did not end with the meeting of PMs, it was followed by a meeting of foreign minister SM Krishna and his Chinese counterpart Yang Jiechi at Bangalore on October 27 after the ninth trilateral meeting between India, Russia and China. In the spirit of Cold Peace, Mr Krishna raised the issues of India's concern with his Chinese counterpart, especially the 'reported Chinese plans to build a dam on the Upper Brahmaputra and China's infrastructure development in Pakistan-occupied Kashmir'.

India is not hesitant in engaging with China on bilateral disputes while at the same time exploring and strengthening the areas of cooperation between the two emerging economies of Asia. This is the message of Dr. Singh's October 25 statement of 'functional cooperation'. Cooperate and compete and make every effort to resolve conflicts between two big neighbouring countries is the essence of India's approach towards China. Incidentally, international law is not helpful on the Chinese desire to construct a dam on the Brahmaputra.

The UN International Convention of 1997 on Non-Navigational Uses of International Water Courses mentions that the lower-riparian country should be consulted and its cooperation should be sought. India abstained in the vote in the UN and China had opposed this Convention of 1997. Because of this, India and China will have to enter into a political dialogue and negotiations on the issue of construction of a dam on Brahmaputra from the Tibetan side. The dust on Brahmaputra has not settled yet and the visit of the Dalai Lama to Arunachal Pradesh from November 8 has heightened the level of public dispute between India and China. Arunachal Pradesh is a bone of contention between the two countries, especially India's claim on Tawang is not acceptable to the Chinese and India rejects China's claim on Arunachal Pradesh by asserting that 'it is an integral part of India.

China expressed dissatisfaction with India on November 9 by stating that 'the Indian side allowed Dalai Lama to visit the disputed eastern section of the China-India border. In reaction, Shashi Tharoor described Chinese statement as an 'irritant'. While India and China are locked in a controversy on Dalai Lama's seven-day visit to Arunachal Pradesh, the Chinese have announced that they will supply $1.5-billion worth arms to Pakistan. Indian public opinion reacts strongly against any country, whether the US or China supplying arms for military build-up of Pakistan. Indians suspect China's special-status relationship with Pakistan.

Thus it is clear that India and China are in a state of Cold Peace where conflicts exist but the mechanism of dialogue is accepted by both the countries for resolving the bilateral disputes. But this is not enough. Policymakers of both the countries cannot ignore the fact that the macro and micro frameworks of political economy of the 21st century have to be kept in mind while dealing with the legacies of the old and dead colonial past. India and China are today big economic players and the western capitalist countries have been compelled to accept that Asia is the centre of new economic power in the 21st century. The Chinese are never tired of proclaiming the new century as an Asian century. Can the Asian century prosper and grow if India and China are at loggerheads?

It deserves to be noted that both India and China have made positive bilateral contribution at the ongoing negotiations on climate change and their united voice will be heard with great attention at the Copenhagen conference on climate change. Not only this, the two countries have also dramatically expanded their bilateral trade relations and, in 2005, India and China had signed the Strategic and Cooperative Partnership for Peace and Prosperity Pact and, in 2008, Dr. Singh and President Hu Jintao had brought out a shared vision document.

Why not concretise these two pacts/documents of 2005 and 2008? Dr. Singh has correctly emphasised that the existing mechanisms for dialogue and discussion between the two countries are adequate enough to deal with contentious issues such as Brahmaputra dam's construction. It should not be forgotten that in a kicking democracy like India's, pro- and anti-China lobbies are always ready to jump at the issue that generates a feeling of ill-will between the two. The Chinese should also keep in mind that their media went overboard on Dalai's visit on November 8 to Arunachal Pradesh and mentioned that India should not forget about 1962. This statement of the Chinese media was simply absurd because both the countries have to accept that 21st century demands that both should act as responsible emerging power centres in Asia.

Both India and China have common stakes and common interests in maintaining peace in Asia to achieve economic growth with social equality. During the phase of Cold Peace, relations between these two countries will be based on stormy debates and also the quest for bilateral cooperation will continue. This is the dialectical reality of India-China relationship.

—21 November, 2009, The Economic Times

A Public Relations Exercise

The Prime Minister's visit to the US was a total failure in terms of a foreign policy mission as he still doesn't realise that America's policies are moulded by its own national interests

The highly publicised official visit of Prime Minister Manmohan Singh to Washington, DC, last month deserves to be closely scrutinised. This is because the UPA, both in its previous avatar and now, has announced that India has developed a 'very special' relationship with the US. The eagerness on the part of the Manmohan Singh Government to sell the idea of 'special India' to the American public and policymakers became clear during Mr Singh's interactions with informal centres of American power like the Council on Foreign Affairs, the US Chamber of Commerce, the US-India Business Council, and through the India-US joint statement issued on November 25.

Though the credibility of joint statements issued after formal meetings between heads of Governments is quite low—this was clearly stated by Minister of State for External Affairs Shashi Tharoor while dismissing the reference to Balochistan in the joint statement issued by the Indian Prime Minister and his Pakistani counterpart Yousuf Raza Gilani at Sharm el-Sheikh—they are representative of the underlying fundamentals in a bilateral relationship.

It is true that Indians were rattled by the joint statement issued by US President Barack Obama and his Chinese counterpart Hu Jintao at the conclusion of their formal meetings from November 15 to 19. But Mr Singh seized the first opportunity to tell the Americans in his address to the Council on Foreign Relations that, "The world had come to terms with the peaceful rise of China ... However, there is a certain assertiveness on the part of China. I am unable to understand it. It should be taken note of." Mr Obama, like his predecessor Mr George W Bush, knows that China is a tough nut to crack.

Given the value of the renminbi vis-à-vis the greenback and China's advantageous trade equation with the US, Mr Obama did not get any concession from the Chinese on his first official visit to Beijing. Hence, the Americans do not need Mr Singh to tell them that new China is assertive.

Mr Singh continued to market the idea of India to the Americans, emphasising that China was no role model for Indians. He stated, "There are values and principles too. China's economic growth has been superior to ours. But India does not want to adopt the Chinese model. We have our own values where human rights, religious freedom, democracy and multiculturalism are appreciated...." He also said that "both India and the US draw strength from their common values..."

Mr Singh is either innocent or naïve because American foreign, economic and strategic policies are not conditioned by the domestic political systems of different countries but are moulded by American national interests. Is Afghan President Hamid Karzai democratically elected? Yet the US wants him at the helm of affairs in Afghanistan. The Americans are not going to change their approach towards China just because India is upset. After all, Mr Obama refused to meet the Dalai Lama because he felt that the Chinese would be offended by such an action. The Americans have hardly been persuaded by Mr Singh and his monologue on the great values of Indian democracy compared to the growing global assertiveness of China.

Mr Singh's second agenda was to clearly convey to Mr Obama that Pakistan, a special friend of the US, is actively engaged in perpetrating terrorism against India and that Washington, DC, should think about a joint anti-terror mechanism with New Delhi. It is one thing on the part of Mr Obama to state that India and the US share a defining partnership of the 21st century, and another to establish a joint front against Pakistan to fight terrorism. Pakistan has always been a frontline state for the Americans, whether during the Cold War era or during the Afghan war.

The US needs Pakistan for its own interests in the Arab world, even if it means the latter misusing American aid to arm itself against India. We will simply have to fight our own battles against Pakistan-sponsored terrorism.

The US is fighting a 'necessary war' in Afghanistan, and without Pakistan's help, American efforts towards exterminating the *jihadis* can never succeed. Mr Singh should know that a neo-imperialist power like the US cannot be expected to be persuaded by India. Hence, Mr Singh's trip can be said to be a total failure in terms of a foreign policy mission. At best, it was an exercise in public relations.

—2 December, 2009, The Pioneer

Worrisome US Policy

AfPak II Takes a Narrow, Restricted View

India's security environment is impacted by developments in Pakistan and Afghanistan and this is the reason why New Delhi should seriously examine the real implications of US President Barack Obama's address on December 1 at the US Military Academy at West Point. His policy statement is the first authentic elaboration of America's thinking on security issues concerning the whole region of South Asia.

The real focus of Mr Obama's policy statement was primarily on Afghanistan and Pakistan. But American actions in these two countries have a direct bearing on the security of India.

Mr Obama said that it was in the national interest of the US to send 30, 000 more troops in addition to the 100, 000 coalition forces that are already stationed because "US security is at stake in Afghanistan". Further, the US cannot undertake 'cleansing' of Al Qaeda or other Muslim fundamentalists like the Taliban without the full cooperation of Pakistan. Hence, Mr Obama in his speech maintained that both Afghanistan and Pakistan are under threat from Al Qaeda, and this is the reason that the US has established a partnership with Pakistan. It is not without reason that Mr Obama's first major foreign policy decision, just after assuming power in January 2009, was to approach the Congress to sanction heavy military and economic aid to Pakistan. The hefty American aid to Islamabad was justified on the basis of the argument that Pakistan was a special 'strategic partner' of the US in the fight against Al Qaeda in Afghanistan.

Mr Obama motivated his soldiers at the US Military Academy by advancing philosophical justification for his commitment to the war against Al Qaeda in Afghanistan. He also told them to take Pakistan along in this 'joint venture'.

America's unilateralist foreign policy of military intervention was justified by Mr Obama by stating that "... we must draw on the strength of our values for the challenges we face may have changed but the things we believe in must not. That is why we must promote our values...". This statement clearly asserts America's self-defined goal of playing the role of a global leader and 'remake' the world in its own image. This is a goal of an imperialist power; to export its 'values of democracy' with the power of the gun.

Washington, DC, may be arming Pakistan on the basis of 'mutuality of interests'. But for India, the latter is the epicentre of terror activities perpetrated against it. Indo-Pak relations continue to be in a trough as Islamabad is not acting against the perpetrators of the 26/11 Mumbai attacks despite the evidence provided by New Delhi in six dossiers.

The indictment of David Coleman Headley for conspiracy in the 26/11 Mumbai attacks by the US Federal Bureau of Investigation and the naming of a retired Pakistani Army Major in the plot have clearly indicated direct involvement of Pakistan-based militants who are supported by the ISI in perpetrating global *jihad*.

Therefore, despite having legitimate interests in the development of Afghanistan, India's role is being obstructed by the great Indo-Pak divide. Apart from providing development aid worth more than $ 1 billion, India is helping train Afghan Army officers, non-commissioned officers and medical personnel.

However, under the present India-Pakistan-Afghanistan situation, New Delhi should keep in mind that its role in Afghanistan is quite limited, even unpredictable, in the near future. It is not surprising that the reason the US has been strengthening the Pakistani Army and calling it a 'dependable ally of America' is that India is not relevant in Mr Obama's strategic approach towards Afghanistan and Pakistan.

However, India cannot be unmindful of American activities in Pakistan and Afghanistan because the withdrawal of American and allied forces from Afghanistan will mean collapse of local political authority in that country. In such a scenario, Pakistan will make every effort to fill the power vacuum in post-America Afghanistan. Hence, India should concentrate on its foreign and security relations with Pakistan and leave Afghanistan to the Americans. The West Point speech of Mr Obama clearly reveals that he is looking at Afghanistan and Pakistan from the perspective of national interest. Therefore, it must be realised that America's military stakes cannot be India's stakes too.

While Pakistan is getting militarily strengthened by receiving American aid, there is no evidence that it has shown any consideration for India after Mr Obama came to power in January 2009. Hence, India has to deal with Pakistan on the basis of its own resources and its own judgement about latter's attitude.

India must reject Mr Obama's revised AfPak strategy which is solely aimed at strengthening the Pakistani Army and involving India in an arm race with Pakistan. A militarily strong Pakistan, supported by the Americans, has less commitment towards Mr Obama's goals in Afghanistan than its own goals against India. Hence, the policymakers should focus on the Indo-Pak relations and not on India's role in Afghanistan.

—15 December, 2009, The Pioneer

Look Beyond America

Basic Countries Show the Way in Copenhagen

As imperialist countries have always been extremely reluctant and hesitant to take any worthwhile step to face the grave challenges posed by global warming at international level, it was good to see Prime Minister Manmohan Singh rescue the sinking ship of the UN climate change summit in Copenhagen.

The parleys at Copenhagen summit should have been an eye-opener for a completely pro-American Manmohan Singh Government that India can actively bargain with the recalcitrant superpower with the cooperation of other non-European emerging economies.

The pro-American UPA Government foreign policymakers should clearly grapple with the fast changing context of international power system and also about the declining power of the US. America has suffered serious setbacks not only because of global economic meltdown but also because its economy is not able to bear the burden of expenditure of trillion of dollars in wars against Iraq and the ongoing war against the Taliban and Al Qaeda in Afghanistan. Even American public opinion has turned against US President Barack Obama's continuing involvement in war in Afghanistan especially at a time when ordinary American citizen is suffering from the adverse effects of recession.

Indian negotiators in Copenhagen would have learnt their two lessons: First, there is a world beyond and without America. Second, it is the US which needs BASIC countries—Brazil, South Africa, India and China. The bloc of these four emerging centres of economic power were sought after by the Americans because of the economic, political and strategic weight these countries have in Latin America, Africa, East Asia and South Asia respectively. It is not the first time that the BASIC countries have discussed their mutual problems and announced their arrival at a global platform. The emergence of the BASIC countries and their desire to work together at the global level clearly shows that America has to deal with 'alternative emerging centres of power'.

The so-called Copenhagen Accord is not at all the result of American dictations as pre-eminent super power. Instead it has a seal of approval of the BASIC countries without whose 'active or passive' consent, the US President would have gone back empty-handed.

Besides, the unity and cooperation shown by India and China at the Copenhagen summit is a very positive development. Relations between these two neighbours can further be strengthened with a view to resolve bilateral disputes and enhance their cooperation of mutual benefit. India and China can compete and cooperate without policies of hostile confrontation and this is the message from Copenhagen.

It has been reported that some European countries are quite worried about the growing spirit of cooperation between India and China as shown by the two Prime Ministers of these countries at the Copenhagen summit. Both the Prime Ministers were in constant touch with each other on negotiations in Copenhagen and this new personal chemistry of trust between these two political executive heads is a very important gain from Copenhagen.

It cannot be denied that some important disputes between these two countries have not be resolved and such lingering of unresolved issues have given birth to mutual suspicions, even hostilities. But this is only one part of the history of India-China relations. However, it is essential for both the countries to catch the bull by the horns and open new avenues of friendship and cooperation in the second decade of the 21st century. It is a well known fact that cooperation between two neighbours especially those with historically inherited disputes, can become the basis of bilateralism only if suspicions are replaced by trust.

The political signals from Copenhagen are quite positive and it is for foreign policymakers to make use of alternative routes to build friendship and cooperation with China. Further, India can build relationship with other Asian countries at the Shanghai Cooperation Organisation Summit. While Russia, China and Central Asian states are member countries of the SCO, India, Iran and Pakistan are important 'observer' countries at the meetings of the Shanghai Cooperation Organisation.

The message from the SCO summit and the Copenhagen meet is that world can be managed and issues can be resolved without the so-called hegemonic presence of imperialist America.

—29 December, 2009

Gen Kayani is a better bet than Gilani

In the Prime Minister's Press conference on May 24, Mr Manmohan Singh uttered some platitudes as to peaceful relations with neighbouring countries being a prerequisite for the economic and social development of India. Mr Singh's statement was made with special reference to Pakistan.

Mr Singh's initiatives for launching negotiations with Pakistan were derailed when in a joint statement at Sharm el-Sheikh at the beginning of his second term as Prime Minister, he and his Pakistani counterpart Yousuf Raza Gilani agreed upon India being prepared to discuss its neighbour's concerns on suspected involvement of the former in Balochistan.

All hell broke loose following the Prime Minister's naïve and uncalled for reference to Balochistan. Mr Singh had to answer extremely inconvenient questions on the matter even while the central issue of the talks and the subsequent discussions should have been the terrorism against India exported from Pakistani territory.

The dust has since settled and the meetings of Foreign Secretaries of India and Pakistan and the proposed meeting between the Foreign Ministers of these two countries are on the UPA Government's agenda. The Prime Minister spelt out the framework for this when he stated at the conference that India "must talk to Pakistan to reduce trust deficit" since "Pakistan is our neighbour. It is my belief that India cannot realise its development potential unless we have the best possible relations with our neighbouring country." He further said that "only future events can say whether or not the dialogue initiative is a success."

Why is there such a serious "trust deficit" between the two neighbouring countries? The causes of this trust deficit have to be clearly identified before any journey for meaningful dialogue and negotiations between these two countries can be undertaken. Mr Singh has to identify and locate the real centre of power in Pakistan because any meaningful dialogue can be undertaken only between those heads of state who have unquestioned political legitimacy in their country. The Prime Minister of India, fully supported by the Parliament, can negotiate with Pakistan without any constraints or unnecessary extra-democratic pressures. The political situation in Pakistan is just the opposite to that of democratic India.

Is President Asif Ali Zardari of the Pakistan's People Party the real wielder of Government authority? Is Mr Gilani of the PPP sufficiently equipped to deal with the complex problems that exist between the two unfriendly neighbours? Is Mr Nawaz Sharif, the unquestioned leader of PML(N), in a position to stand by his Prime Minister? What is the status of Pakistan Army chief Gen Ashfaq Parvez Kayani in the corridors of power? Indians need to be reminded that when Prime Minister Atal Bihari Vajpayee was being welcomed by then Prime Minister Nawaz Sharif, Gen Pervez Musharraf, the then Army chief, had his troops invade Kargil heights which led to a war between India and Pakistan. Mr Sharif, as the Prime Minister, had publicly stated after his ouster that Gen Musharraf had acted on his own, without informing or consulting the Prime Minister.

This adequately demonstrates that the military establishment in Pakistan can independently play a decisive role with respect to India or Afghanistan. The elected political leadership of Pakistan does not exercise any control over the autonomous functioning of its military and the ISI under the protection and patronage of which anti-India terrorist groups are operating.

The United States has always paid lip service to Pakistan's political class and worked through Pakistani Army for the protection of its own interests whether in Afghanistan or against Taliban groups operating from Pakistan. That they have sufficient clout over Pakistan's military establishment has been proved by the involvement of its Army in the fight against Taliban forces in Waziristan.

It is not without reason that Gen Kayani, during his visit to the US along with the Prime Minister, was seen negotiating the quantum of military aid to Pakistan by the Obama Administration. It is a part of recorded history that the US is more comfortable dealing with the military-guided and controlled formal democracy of Pakistan than the vibrant and noisy democracy of India.

Do Indians have any lessons to learn from the nature of US diplomacy with Pakistan? India and Pakistan are bound by history and geography and a *modus vivendi* must be found to resolve the disputes between them without interfering in one another's domestic affairs. India should identify interlocutors to bring Pakistan's military establishment to the table for negotiations. Political dialogue should continue but if India wants a real solution to bilateral disputes, it should engage in meaningful talks with Pakistan's military establishment, following in the footsteps of other nations.

—1 June, 2010, The Pioneer

Needed, a Foreign Policy Review

Bilateral conflicts between South Asian nations have impacted the development of the whole region. India and Pakistan are victims of a serious 'trust deficit' and the adversarial relationship between the two neighbouring countries has affected the security environment of the subcontinent.

The long civil war waged in Sri Lanka exercised an extremely negative influence in India because the Tamils of Sri Lanka had a natural ethnic constituency in Tamil Nadu the social fabric of which was completely vitiated by the internal strife on the island. Political parties in Tamil Nadu pressurised the Government of India to intervene in the ongoing civil war and protect the Tamil fraternity resulting in Rajiv Gandhi taking a disastrous step by sending out the Indian Peace Keeping Force.

The porous border of Bangladesh is used not only by illegal migrants but is also a safe sanctuary for insurgent groups of the North-East. The Union Government is forced to engage in dialogue with the Government of Bangladesh so as not to allow refuge to hostile anti-India groups on its soil. The Maoists of Nepal consider India as their enemy and allege that India interferes in the political process of their country. The conflict situation in South Asia has been aggravated by the involvement of Americans and NATO forces in the war against Taliban in Afghanistan.

The nine-year war, launched by the US in 2001 with a 1,30,000-strong Army against the Taliban, has changed the geopolitical landscape of the South Asian region because India, Pakistan, Iran and even China have been compelled to rethink and review their strategies in the light of the results of this war. South Asian countries must recognise that the fate of the region is tied together and bilateral and multilateral conflicts with each other have an adverse impact on the economic and security environment of the region. Such recognition will act as a catalyst for the resolution of bilateral conflicts and promote areas of cooperation among the countries of this region. Second, any involvement of an outside superpower has helped only to exacerbate conflicts among the nation-states. US policies have created a 'trust deficit' between India and Pakistan. They have led to an endless arms race between the two countries. Pakistan's military buildup, which is directed only against India, has been the sole contribution of the US.

The most recent example of adverse consequences of American involvement in South Asian politics is provided by the ongoing war in Afghanistan. Pakistan has increased its political and strategic clout in Afghanistan by actively allying with the US in this war. Pakistan is not worried at all about the fact that the US cannot win this war. The Taliban is very secure in Pakistan. They are not opposed to the Pakistani state or its strategic interests in Afghanistan. The tottering regime of Mr Hamid Karzai is forced to negotiate with the Taliban to deal with the post-war vacuum in the country.

US president Barack Obama has given marching orders to Gen Stanley McChrystal, the commander of NATO forces, and appointed Gen David H Petraeus in his place as a face-saving exercise. Mr Obama has decided to withdraw NATO troops from Afghanistan in 2011. A destabilised Afghanistan divided into Pashtun, Uzbek, Tajik and Hazara communities will be involved in inter-clan warfare because the Taliban as well as Mr Karzai, himself, belong to the Pashtun tribe and a lot of atrocities have earlier been committed against Uzbeks, Tajiks and Hazaras. The Americans and NATO forces will leave Afghanistan as they left Iraq—in chaos.

Pakistan is the only beneficiary of the war in Afghanistan and it is fully prepared to play a critical and central role in post-war Afghanistan. Indian policymakers had hoped for a longer US stay in Afghanistan in vain and wholeheartedly supported the war. It is never too late to rethink policy options. Referring to Iran, Indian Foreign Secretary Nirupama Rao stated on July 5, "We are both neighbouring countries of Afghanistan and Pakistan and have long suffered from the threat of transitional terrorism originating from beyond our borders."

The India-Iran Joint Commission meeting is being held when 'a rapidly changing matrix' in Afghanistan is a concern for both these countries. It is a well known fact that Iran is a Shia regime. India should actively engage with Iran because of their 'commonality of interests' in Afghanistan.

—14 June, 2010, The Pioneer

Asian Century: Cooperation or Conflict?

The dream of an Asian century cannot be realised till India, China and Japan arrive at a mutual understanding and abandon the path of resolving historical disputes through military competitiveness.

Statesmen, public policymakers and transnational financial institutions and reputed credit rating and fund-giving agencies of the advanced capitalist countries are asserting that the erstwhile underdeveloped Asia has left behind its status of the Third World.

The 21st century has been heralded as the age of Asia that is marching forward, and the rate of economic growth of emerging Asian giants like China and India is much more than that of the US and EU. A few important facts can be mentioned to substantiate the argument that the Western capitalist countries are looking at Asia much more closely.

First, General Motors Corp managing director stated on July 5, 2010, that 'We know that to remain a global leader, we have to maintain our commitment to expanding GM's presence and success in critical markets such as India and China'.

Second, the International Monetary Fund (IMF) and World Bank had always been acting as 'watchdogs' of the fate of Asian economies, and in the first decade of the 21st century, these two institutions have become quite euphoric about the rate of economic growth and bright future of Asia. The IMF has projected 9.4 per cent growth for India during January-December, and it is second only to China's at 10.5 per cent. The IMF has projected that the world's rate of growth during 2010 may be 4.6 per cent and global economies have been pulled out of the grand recession of 2008 because China and India have performed quite well.

Third, the erstwhile Asian markets that were completely dependent for investments and aid for trade on the Western capitalist countries have now become global players and they are not only making investments in the US and European markets, but are also actively engaged in acquisitions of Western companies.

Thus, it has become appropriate to describe the present situation as being Asia's century. It has led even World Bank president Robert Zoellick to declare that '2009 saw the end of what was known as the Third World'.

The other perspective is that Asians are plagued with serious domestic challenges of the eradication of mass poverty. Not only China and India, but many Asian countries such as Thailand, Pakistan, Myanmar, Nepal et al are tied down with violent domestic social challenges, and in many Asian countries, social unrest has spread to an extent that the institutional authority of the state is under siege.

The majority of the nation-states of Asia still have to establish their legal authority over their socially-discontented and volatile sections. If on the one hand, emerging Asian countries are facing serious challenges arising out of conflicts and acute social divisions within their own societies, on the other, the whole continent of Asia is engaged in inter-state bilateral and multilateral disputes that have many a time led to actual war or war-like situations.

The idea of peaceful co-existence and mutual cooperation talked about by Jawaharlal Nehru and Chou-en-Lai in the 1950s was abandoned by both India and China in the 1962 Sino-Indian war. Both the countries still have a high level of mutual distrust, even compete lack of confidence.

The reality is that both are competing against one another for extending their areas of influence around the world. It deserves to be clearly stated that Asia is confronted with a serious challenge from nuclear weapon states like China, India, Pakistan and North Korea.

This dangerous nuclearisation of Asia is sufficient evidence to substantiate the argument that Asian countries are competing against one another and are taking recourse to military power for resolving their inter-state bilateral disputes, many of which have been inherited from their colonial past.

The EU took shape only after forgetting the memories of their past mutual conflicts and wars. After WWII, Europe was divided into hostile Cold War blocs, and with the end of Cold War, moves started for establishing unity in highly-diverse Europe. The moral of this story is that possibilities of peaceful co-existence with a spirit of mutuality and reciprocity cannot be achieved in Asia because its countries are guided by the spirit of distrust and the historical memories of the colonial phase of its history has not faded out of Asia.

The best example of mutual distrust among Asian countries is provided by Shanghai Cooperation Organization that consists of members such as China, Russia, Kazakhstan, Kyrgyzstan, Tajikistan and Uzbekistan.

Countries like India and Pakistan that have legitimate stakes in Asian cooperation have been kept out by China, the originator of the idea of the Shanghai Cooperation Organization.

The idea of an Asian age cannot become a reality unless India, China and Japan arrive at a level of mutual understanding and abandon the path of resolving historical disputes on the basis of military competitiveness. This is a time of great opportunities for Asia if India and China can come to terms with one another with a spirit of accommodation and cooperation.

China and India reciprocate negatively to any action by any of the countries perceived to be a challenge to their security. India reacted very strongly against China when it vetoed the loan for Arunachal Pradesh, which was to be approved by the Asian Development Bank in 2009.

China and India have not reached a state of mutual trust where they can bury their border disputes inherited from the past. India scrutinises every action of China when it supports the building of the armed forces of Pakistan. The Chinese defence minister stated on June 16, 2010, that 'Cooperation between the Chinese and Pakistani armed forces is exemplary and has been fruitful'.

Further, the level of distrust between two large counties of Asia increased when China raised the level of military cooperation with Pakistan or when it laid claim on the Indian state of Arunachal Pradesh.

The above narrative highlights that unlike the idea of an American century or the age of European unity, Asia cannot graduate to the levels of stable Western centres of power because the growing economic power of Asian countries is a necessary, but not a sufficient, condition for Asians to emerge as a centre of power.

Asian countries are saddled with serious domestic problems of poverty, inequality and social strife. And with mutual relations among these countries being based on distrust and conflicts, Asia has miles to go before it can become a real centre of power in the global context.

—24 July, 2010, The Economic Times

Why UPA2 must Revise Talks Strategy

A sea change is taking place in the war situation in Afghanistan. On August 4 during his visit to France, Pakistan's President Asif Ali Zardari said, "I believe the international community, which Pakistan belongs to, is in the process of losing the war against the Taliban." It is an authoritative statement by the President of a country actively involved in the internal affairs of Afghanistan and such an assessment is bound to make the Pakistani state evolve its own approach by keeping it own future national interests in mind in the post-war situation in Afghanistan.

It is a well-known fact that different Taliban factions enjoy a comfortable and safe sanctuary in Pakistan's Waziristan and Balochistan. British Prime Minister David Cameron, during his visit to India, warned Pakistan not to "export terrorism" from its country's soil either to neighbouring countries or other countries in the world. Mr Cameron also sternly warned Pakistan that it should be "prepared to face international isolation" if it continues to follow this policy.

Following the WikiLeaks disclosure, the US Administration has suffered a loss of face. Americans have not publicly admitted so but they have given many messages to Pakistan to 'act as an honest ally of America' in war in Afghanistan. It deserves to be clearly stated that America has been taken for a ride by Pakistan, pretending to be an 'ally' in war against Taliban from 2001 to 2010. Pakistan always had its own interests in Afghanistan and that neighbouring country has always been an important factor in Pakistan's overall security and other strategic calculations for the last 60 years. The Afghan policy has occupied a central place in Pakistan's overall strategic thinking irrespective of changing regimes whether in Pakistan or Afghanistan. Incidentally, it is not only Americans, but even Afghan President Hamid Karzai, himself a Pashtun, is also thinking of policy options towards Taliban in a post-war situation. Mr Karzai has already opened convert dialogue with so-called 'good Taliban'.

The Taliban are likely to return to power which they lost due to the American-led aggression against them. The time has come for the Pakistani Government to open its policy cards towards Afghanistan. The first pillar of Pakistan's Afghan policy is to completely 'eject' India from the country. Canadian Ambassador to Kabul, Mr Chris Alexander, from 2003-2005, stated on August 2, that "the Inter-Services Intelligence is the main driver of the conflict in Afghanistan" and Pakistan's goal is to "close all Indian consulates in Islamic Emirates of Afghanistan". The main architect of the new Pakistani policy towards post-war Afghanistan is Army chief Gen Ashfaq Parvez Kayani whose term has been extended for three more years.

In pursuit of the anti-India Kashmir-centred policy, Pakistan has completely betrayed the Americans in Afghanistan by openly supporting, even allying with, Maulana Jalaluddin Haqqani whom the Americans want to crush. US Secretary of Defence Robert Gates stated on August 3 that the "operation could be on Al Qaeda on both sides of the border" and the reference is to Pakistan and Afghanistan where Al Qaeda and Haqqani supporters are concentrated. Mr Gates' statement clearly shows the US' frustration with Pakistan's role in liquidating Taliban who are operating from within its own territory. After the US' website's leak of documents, the US must admit their knowledge of Pakistan's double game.

India has been crying itself hoarse at all international fora about the active involvement of Pakistan in prompting terrorism against India from its own territory. The Americans need not have waited to know about this basic fact. The US wants a "decisive push by Pakistan against terrorists, especially Haqqani supporters, who have safe havens close to the borders of Pakistan". Not to be left behind, Mr Karzai on July 29 "urged western allies to destroy Islamist militant sanctuaries in neighbouring Pakistan". Is the US helpless in a situation of its own creation? When the US invested every resource in Pakistan and built its Army, it forgot that a neo-colonial state could become 'relatively autonomous' of its benefactor and promoter as every state, howsoever dependent it may be on a superpower, has some national goals of its own.

Pakistan's only interest in Afghanistan was to support the American war and establish a *quid pro quo* for receiving large scale military aid to increase its own strength to pursue its anti-India Kashmir policies and quietly penetrate in Afghanistan and establish its own autonomous zone of influence in that country. The US war in Afghanistan beginning from 2001 to 2010 has proved beneficial to Pakistan.

Further, the US, in the second decade of the 21st century, is retreating as a defeated power from Afghanistan. This has provided further space to

Pakistan to operate on its own in South Asia. The changing regional scenario has a clear message. Indian interests in Afghanistan are at stake. More importantly, India's fight against Pakistan-based terrorist groups is now linked to its own capabilities and it will receive little help save lip service in this respect from other nations. India has to reckon with this new reality and deal and negotiate with Pakistan on the basis of its own bilateral resources. It should not own expect any help from the US while making its policy calculations with respect to Pakistan.

—10 August, 2010, The Pioneer

Kashmir: Victim of Vested Interests

The stone-throwing violent activity ostensibly led by the so-called alienated and disgruntled youth of the Kashmir Valley has once again brought into sharp focus the continuing abnormal political situation in the state. The central government, along with the state's established political leaders, has made efforts to provide temporary healing touch to the dissatisfied sections of Kashmiri society and efforts have been made to find a lasting solution to the Kashmir problem.

Prime Minister Manmohan Singh convened a meeting of every political group and parties on August 10, 2010, and appealed to the Kashmiris to give 'peace a chance', and urged the stone-throwing youth to 'go back to their studies' and promised to tackle the economic problems of Kashmir with emphasis on 'employment-generation opportunities', especially for the youth.

The prime minister also made a commitment to reopen dialogue to address the demand for more autonomy 'within the framework of the Constitution of India'. It deserves to be stated that Manmohan Singh's predecessors too took initiatives to tackle the Kashmiri demand for autonomy to satisfy their local aspirations. Why is it that no dialogue or negotiation between the central government and Kashmiri political groups resulted in the restoration of normalcy and peace in the Valley?

If the lack of economic development has made the Kashmiris angry, India has enough fiscal resources for special developmental schemes for Kashmir. It is a facile explanation to maintain that violence-ridden conflict situation exists in the Valley because people feel deprived because of lack of economic development.

PDP's Mehbooba Mufti, All-Party Hurriyat Conference chairman Mirwaiz Umar Farooq and Tahreek-e-Hurriyat's Syed Ali Gilani expressed their sharp differences with the prime minister's approach and refused to be party to negotiations on the autonomy issue with the central government or economic package offered by the central government. Dukhtaran-e-Millat leader Asiya Andrabi said that Kashmiris are not beggars. Why did Mehbooba Mufti, whose party participates in the electoral process, refuse to become an active partner in all-party negotiations with the central government?

Hence, the real reason for continuing conflict that has often become violent during the last 62 years is not lack of transfer of fiscal resources by the Centre. The central government has lavishly funded all disturbed regions and sub-regions , not only Kashmir but also the north-east , and it is a cry of the wolf to suggest that underdevelopment and lack of economic opportunities in insurgency-inflicted regions are responsible for insurgency. The alternative explanation to the failure of the central government to find a permanent solution for conflict-ridden regions is that very powerful political vested interests are operating in insurgency-hit areas and they are beneficiaries of the turmoil in these states.

It is a known fact that the current violence in Kashmir originated with the kidnapping of Rubaiya Sayeed on December 8, 1989, whose father, the then-Union home minister Mufti Mohammad Sayeed, made Indian state 'bend and beg' of the militants to release his daughter, and militant groups in the Valley concluded that the Indian state can be forced to surrender to blackmail.

The militants had a field day and they indulged in ethnic cleansing and many new militant groups like Muslim Mujahedeen et alwere born that intensified anti-India militant activities. Pakistani army and Inter-Services Intelligence are actively involved in the massive funding of militancy and terrorism in Kashmir with a view to achieve its longcherished goal of destabilising India by delinking Kashmir. It is not only that Pakistan has a clear vested interest in keeping Kashmir Valley disturbed, many factions and groups are liberally funded and patronised by Pakistan to keep the pot boiling in Kashmir.

Many political groups and leaders, openly or in a clandestine manner, are playing the Pakistani card in Kashmir on the basis of quid pro quo with an obliging Pakistan to fill the coffers of these self-appointed 'separatists' who know that the Indian state can never allow reterritorisation of Jammu and Kashmir and hand it over to Pakistan. The Pakistan-funded pro-Azadi groups operate in India and block the process of normalisation in the Valley because if normal political process is not disturbed, these pro-Azadi mercenary leaders and groups lose their heavy pocket money from Pakistan.

It is not only the well-identified Azadi groups led by Gilani or Lone or Asiya Andrabi of the Dukhtaran-e-Millat or jihadi or Islamic fundamentalists who are a road block in the way of normalcy in Kashmir, political parties wielding power in the state also raise extremist demands and compel the nervous central government to extend extra favour and patronage to such parties that use democratic forum to air their extremist demands. It deserves to be clearly stated that parties like PDP, a Mufti family outfit, participates in the democratic process, occupies the chair of chief minister, and in opposition, plays every trick of the trade to pressure the Centre to directly deal with Mehbooba by ignoring chief minister Omar Abdullah.

The ruling families of the state have taken contradictory and extremist positions vis-avis the central government with a view to gain advantage, whether in power or out of it. Why should PDP work for normalcy in the Valley? Normalcy does not bring a special benefit to the Mufti family and other groups such as the PDP. Ved Marwah, a loyal servant of the Indian state, in his book *India in Turmoil*, states that democratically-elected state governments of disturbed states or foreignfunded insurgents are not interested in normalcy because 'it would bring them out of business' created by militancy.

Terrorism, insurgency, militancy and jihad have all become profitable business for extortion, illegal sale of narcotics and arms. Not to be left behind, the violence-ridden state governments, elected democratically, also have a lion's share in the booty provided by the exchequer. Every road building contract brings financial profit to democratically-elected governments and the insurgent groups. Hence, the Centre keeps on announcing economic packages in the belief that lack of economic development has created the milieu for social discontent.

Hence, roadblocks are those that are within the Indian state system. Kashmir needs a healing touch and launching of Samjhauta Express and a bus to unite the divided families was expected to satisfy the aspirations of the people across the border. Nothing happened.

Mercenary outfits will never allow return of normalcy because it would end their business of politics for fiscal benefits.

—21 August, 2010, The Economic Times

LoC as De Jure Border is a Possible Solution

The visit of an all-Party delegation to Jammu and Kashmir was very significant because only such a step by the national and regional parties from outside Jammu and Kashmir could provide a healing touch to the victims of ongoing conflict in the Valley. The major advantage of such an all-party visit was tall leaders from outside Jammu and Kashmir could collectively convey a clear message to the Kashmiris that the whole country cared about them and was interested in finding solutions to the vexed and complicated Kashmir dispute. Further, this all-party visit provided an opportunity to leaders—especially to that of regional parties who have a very peripheral and superficial understanding of the genesis of the dispute—to observe the Kashmir reality from close quarters. On the other hand, the local leaders and civil society got a chance to convey to the visiting leaders their actual feelings, the problems they faced and what aggravated people at the grass roots level. The post-visit consultations and discussions among the parties and leaders led to the concretisation of Government responses and on September 27, 2010 the Government of India announced an '8-point package for valley peace'. Such a first step by the Central Government has not created any controversy or dissent among the national and regional parties whose leaders visited Jammu and Kashmir.

It is essential to describe the 'Eight-Point Peace Packages' before embarking on any critical analysis of the usefulness or limitations of such a peace package. The Union Government on September 27, announced that it will hold dialogue with the Kashmiris. A day after the peace proposal was announced, the Prime Minister also asked for a report on employment-generating programmes undertaken in Kashmir. It deserves to be stated that the Union Government had appointed 'interlocutors' in the past, but no progress was made in spite of messages conveyed by the interlocutors. Will it be a repeat story of the past? It may not be the case this time, although Syed Ali Shah Geelani, allegedly involved in mobilising the stone-pelting youth, described the initiative as 'eyewash'. Home Minister P Chidambaram has announced that these interlocutors would be under the leadership of eminent persons—probably a 'non-Congress' leader would lead the interlocutors. It is quite clear that the Government wants an all-party consensus and with the political credibility and high status of interlocutors 'such a dialogue' with all sections of Jammu and Kashmir society would carry weight and conviction. This is a break from the past when interlocutors were appointed on the basis of their proximity to the ruling party or coalition.

Further, the ruling and the Opposition parties in Jammu and Kashmir have jointly asked for the withdrawal of the Armed Forces Special Powers Act or limit its applicability only to a notified 'disturbed area'. It is important to understand that long-term deployment of armed forces including paramilitary forces in any region of India, whether Jammu and Kashmir or North East, armed with special laws like AFSPA creates a lot of inconvenience for the local population and in turn, breeds hostility against the men in Khaki. Hence, the prolonged presence of the armed forces has been a vexing reason among a large section of the local population in Kashmir Valley. Hence, Mr Chidambaram stated on September 27: "The notifications have been made under the Jammu and Kashmir Armed Forces Special Powers Act. However, as a matter of prudence and practice, these decisions are taken after the unified command advises the State Government. Therefore, we will request the State Government to convene a meeting of the unified command and review their deployment, review the notifications. So let us wait for them to do the review first."

It is pertinent to bring here the whole context of Kashmir dispute to understand that in spite of grievances and complaints of the local population, Army and paramilitary forces have to be stationed to fight an undeclared war launched by Pakistan against India with a view to unite Kashmiris under the control of the Pakistani state. The Kashmir problem has remained complex due to inept and directionless handling of the situation by the Union Government of India. The Centre and its nominees, the State Governors, have dismissed Jammu and Kashmir elected Governments in the past for purely personal and partisan purposes. Many a time, the Governors were from outside the State, who tried to follow their personal agendas without the support and consent of the elected Governments. Then, State Assembly elections were 'rigged'. Real elected democratic Governments in Jammu and Kashmir have been in power only after the developments of mid-Nineties. The Government of India, beginning with the BJP-led NDA and followed by Manmohan Singh-led UPA, have functioned within a democratic framework. This is the opportune moment to deal with Jammu and Kashmir by working through democratic processes as solutions offered by the Union Government will carry more conviction. It is for the elected representatives of Jammu and Kashmir to politically isolate the separatist and mobilise their own social constituencies to create normalcy for economic development.

The central Government is responsible for dealing with external interventionists in Kashmir. The western powers keep mum regarding Pakistan interference because they have been always dependent on Pakistan Army to fight battles on their behalf. US President Barack Obama has always stated that a 'stable Pakistan' is in the interest of the western Governments. What has the American President to offer Pakistan as a *quid pro quo* for its support in Afghanistan war except Kashmir? The Pakistan Army knows that they cannot occupy Indian territories through a war and they know America cannot dictate any terms to India despite the two countries coming together over the civil nuclear deal. The only solution to Kashmir is that India and Pakistan have to recognise the Line of Actual Control and make borders of two separated Kashmir really 'soft' and easy for travel and trade on both sides of the Line. The moment Pakistan Army realises the futility of war with India for re-territorialisation of Kashmir, the Geelanis, the Lones, the Mirwaizs would collapse like a house of cards. And then, the democratically-elected representatives of Jammu and Kashmir and the Union Government can resolve any conflict in that part of the country.

—4 October, 2010, The Pioneer

The Dualism Obama Represents

It has been repeatedly asserted by the Manmohan Singh government that India has developed a very special strategic partnership with the US and that it has been further strengthened by the prime minister's personal relationship with American presidents like George Bush and Barack Obama. Americans have also reciprocated by emphasising that they are 'natural allies' of democratic India. These statements, made either by the American or Indian foreign and strategic policymakers, are sugar-coated sentiments conveying nothing of substance.

Every country is guided by its own national interests and there is no place for permanent friends or enemies while dealing with concrete issues of bilateral or multilateral international relationships. It should not be forgotten that America is interested in promoting its business interests, especially given that India has emerged as a big market for American commodities.

A report by the Centre for a New American Security called 'National allies: A blueprint for the future of US-India relations' suggested that the "US modify its export control measures... permitting increased exports of defence-related technology and goods to India". This is the main objective of the promotion of the bilateral relationship by characterising it a very special strategic partnership between the US and India.

The same sentiment was authoritatively expressed by US under secretary for political affairs William Burns on October 21, 2010 that the US and India were talking on 'adapting and reforming' US export laws so that 'India can be treated as a partner and not as a target'.

Clearly, 'the business of America is to do business' and it seems immature on our part to celebrate the emerging relationship as very 'special' only for India. American presidents have always been promoters of the business interests of their own countrymen. American multinational corporations collect funds for presidential elections in return for promotion of their business interests at a global level. While trade and business is only one part of the story, the other side is security and the defence interests of India. Which, in effect, the Americans are completely insensitive to.

A few days ago, defence minister AK Antony publicly stated that India's 'security environment has become worrisome'. Army chief General VK Singh, too, has said on October 24 that Pakistan and China are 'major irritants' and 'India was ready to fight a conventional war in a nuclear scenario'.

A few facts deserve to be mentioned to substantiate the argument that America is arming Pakistan on the specious plea of fighting the Taliban. Pakistan has already secured around $7.5 billion under the Kerry-Lugar aid Bill for five years. And on October 22, the US also announced $2.29 billion as military aid to Pakistan. It is ironical for Indians that the 'natural ally' is unmindful of their security concerns. It is utopian to believe that the Americans will help India in the fight against terrorism originating from Pakistan, whose reach now extends to Mumbai and Pune.

Further, Pakistan has no interest in fighting the Taliban and Al Qaeda in Afghanistan because in post-NATO Kabul, Pakistan will have a friendly regime. Indians should forget about any role in post-NATO Afghanistan because neither Pakistan nor the Taliban would allow an Indian presence there. The only contribution of the Americans in South Asia after their withdrawal from Afghanistan will be to leave a well-armed and well-equipped Pakistan.

If these are the realities of geostrategic issues, there should be some weighty reason that India and America are hyperbolic about their relations. The Centre for a New American Security has argued that "a growing closeness between India and the US was important because although neither sought the containment of China, the likelihood of a peaceful Chinese rise increases if it ascends in a region where the great democratic powers are strong."

This remark and also statements from the American state department clearly posit China as a factor in the Asian power system. Indian policymakers have always brushed under the carpet the China factor in an evolving Asia while the Americans have made it public that India and China are important and inter-related areas of operation, cooperation and conflict. Indians would be foolhardy if they allow any role for the Americans as their interlocutor with China. India and China have enough resources of their own to resolve their mutual concerns.

Clearly, America is pursuing its own economic and strategic goals in South Asia and business with India is a priority because of it's an emerging market. The US security interests can be taken care of by Pakistan even if it adversely affects India. In brief, much should not be read into Obama's visit.

—30 October, 2010, The Economic Times

It's Time to Emerge out of America's Shadow

US President Barack Obama's oration and the peroration in his speech to Parliament and a joint statement issued after the completion of his visit provide enough indications to substantiate that in spite of all the noises made by him and Prime Minister Manmohan Singh, India's basic security concerns will continue to occupy the central place in India's own strategic priorities. The priority area of India's strategic concern continues to remain the prevailing situation in South Asia, especially the bilateral relationship with Pakistan, the developing situation in Afghanistan, and the role China decides to play in South Asia.

Mr Obama sermonised on November 7, 2010, that these should be '*détente*' in South Asia and he clearly stated that '.....India has biggest stake in ensuring a secure, stable Pakistan'. Mr Obama further clearly articulated that American position on India and Pakistan would only be that of 'a friend and partner'. And it was '... for the two countries to arrive at their own understanding in terms of how the relationship evolves' Mr Obama has put the ball in India's court by stating that 'it is in your interest that at a time when you are starting to succeed in incredible ways on the global economic stage that you want security and stability in your region'.

It is simplistic to accept that Americans have been unaware of Pakistan's state policy of 'exporting terrorist attack' to India, especially after the attacks in Mumbai on November 26, 2008. Further, David Headley must have given a lot of information to the Americans about the direct involvement of the Pakistani state apparatus in promoting 'terror attacks' against India. There can be only two plausible explanations for America's incapacity or unwillingness to pressurise Pakistan to abandon its policy of 'export of terrorism'. First, America is deeply involved in containing and defeating the Taliban and Al Qaeda armed groups in Afghanistan and in the pursuit of this war in Afghanistan, American and NATO forces require full support from Pakistan. Mr Manmohan Singh may claim 'special friendship' with Mr Obama or Indians may like to live in a make-belief world of 'special strategic partnership' with America, the reality is war in Afghanistan cannot be fought without the full support of

Pakistan and Pakistani leadership is not stupid enough not to reap rich dividends from America.

Mr Obama's predecessor, Mr George W Bush in his memoir *Decision Days* admits that Americans were taken for a ride by the duplicity of General Pervez Musharraf, the former head of the Pakistani military regime. Mr Obama's generous statements in Delhi might have pleased the already converted 'friend' Mr Manmohan Singh, the ground reality has not changed. India's anxieties about the disturbed situation in the South-Asian region have not and cannot be addressed by Mr Obama. It is essential to refer here that with the emergence of the Republicans in the recent mid-term elections, Obama Administration will be forced to continue the war in Afghanistan; and longer the war continues, greater would be the dependence of the American and NATO forces on Pakistan. The Pakistani Army, the real epicentre of power in Pakistan, has always militarily strengthened itself with the assistance of the US, while the Americans were engaged in war in Afghanistan—be it with the erstwhile Soviet Russia or the Taliban and Al Qaeda.

The American shadow over India and Pakistan has impacted the bilateral relationships between these two countries irrespective of the changes in American politics. Since Pakistan was a military ally of America during the Cold War days, the Americans had directly intervened in the Kashmir dispute in support of Pakistan and helped Pakistan fight the war against India supplying American war machines.

The end of Cold War has not brought back normalcy in India-Pakistan bilateral relationship because American shadow still hovers over the region and Pakistan has now become a strategic base for America's war in Afghanistan. Mr Obama may proclaim that bilateral disputes between these two countries have to be resolved by them alone, the reality is that America had haunted and continues to haunt the India-Pakistan relationship over the Kashmir dispute. As long as war in Afghanistan continues, Pakistan has no compulsion to change its approach towards India.

Thus, Mr Obama's visit to India has not brought any relief to Indians either on the issues of export of terrorism or the Kashmir dispute, except some empty phrases. Further, Mr Obama's rhetoric for a need for '*détente* in South Asia' fails to grapple with the reality of China-India-Pakistan relationship. It is a well-known fact that America's clout over China is on the decline and the US itself is engaged in resolving difficult problems with rising China, ready to disturb its apple cart in South China sea and the regional balance of power. It is not without reason that Mr Obama did not come out openly on issues concerning China which have a direct bearing on 'détente in South Asia'.

The regional strategic problems of South Asia demand a careful agenda by India, Pakistan and China and America has no role to play in the resolution of either bilateral relations or in making South Asia a zone of peace. Rather, America's shadow over the South Asia region has always vitiated the atmosphere and Mr Obama has also failed to improve the climate of peace in and around India. It is for Indians to fight their own battles and define their own goals.

—15 November, 2010, The Pioneer

Checkmating China Needs Serious Engagement

If India's response to China's policy announcements, pronouncements or actions is guided by a simplistic or ideologically driven analysis, then it will be counterproductive. India-China relationship is not determined by the single factor of security and strategic consideration, but other factors of mutual interest as well. Apart from being largest trade partners, India and China meet quite frequently, being members of BRIC, to discuss problems of mutual interest.

China's first foreign policy goal is to assert its new-found economic and military power while dealing with the US. Its state actors are quite conscious of their new status in world affairs. The Americans had to plead for Chinese intervention in the recent Korean peninsula stand off because without China's restraining power over North Korea, the conflict between the two Koreas could lead to a devastating war. China considers itself not only a competitor but also capable of checkmating any expansionist or interventionist policies of America. It should not be forgotten that the US is not used to any such challenge from any country in the so-called 'unipolar' world. So it is difficult for the Americans to digest the new reality of power shift in favour of China. China's priority is to contain American influence in world affairs and completely change the balance of global power from America-dominated world to multi-polar global system where it can act as a strong counterveiling force while dealing with the US. India-China bilateral relationship has to be contextualised by keeping in mind that China is focussed on containing the US, especially in Asia, and in its strategic calculation India occupies a central place.

China targeted India in the 1950s and 1960s because it started perceiving India as anti-China following the granting of asylum to Dalai Lama. Thus, the bilateral relationship after the 1962 India-China war was completely frozen till 1970s. Such a situation benefitted Pakistan the most. Pakistan's active engagement with China got an impetus when it facilitated the secret visit of Mr Henry Kissinger and Mr Richard Nixon to China in the early 1970s.

The special relationship between the two countries has further cemented because Pakistan has been benefiting from its dependence on China. China has helped in Pakistan's military build-up, in enhancing its nuclear power capabilities, and it has sided with Pakistan on its Jammu and Kashmir dispute with India. Not only Pakistan has seceded a part of Kashmir's territory to China but also depends on its clandestine support to needle India on the issue of Jammu and Kashmir. It is not without reason that Pakistan President Asif Ali Zardari during his latest visit to China observed that 'coming to China is like home coming' for him. On its part, China has also played the Pakistan card against India whenever it has felt necessary to restrict India.

This is one foreign policy reality that should directly affect India's responses towards China. Pakistan can effectively influence China's actions at the international fora. In the past, it had succeeded through China's intervention in the UN Security Council to stop the international body from imposing sanctions against terrorist organisations like Jamaat-ud-Dawa'h of Hafiz Saeed.

Further, China is asserting its maritime rights especially in South China Sea. It is also building dams on the Brahmaputra river from the side of Tibet and India is worried about the water issues which can emerge after the dams have been constructed. India is a lower riparian state and expects the Chinese to safeguard water interests while constructing dams on Brahmaputra.

Apart from the boundary issue that continues to divide the two neighbours, there are some serious doubts among the Indians about China's South Asia policy and China reciprocates the same feelings of suspicion towards India. China suspects that American-Indian axis is emerging to contain its rising influence in Asia. On the other hand, India, a victim of state-sponsored terrorism, finds China's support to Pakistan on Taliban and Al Qaeda terrorist groups is aimed at destabilising India. Though China has never supported Pakistan military in its wars against India, but it definitely enjoys a special relationship with Pakistan.

Though Prime Minister Manmohan Singh has publicly tried to remove Chinese doubts by asserting that 'there is enough space in the world for these two big countries', the two countries still have to deal with some complex issues to move ahead. India-China relationship cannot be seen with binary perspective because many inter-dependencies exist between these two neighbours. Since these two countries have to co-exist as neighbours, diplomacy should never become a tool in the hands of committed ideologues who see things only in black and white. China and India, being two rising powers in Asia, should bring their relationship to a level where differences could be resolved around the table and mutual suspicions could be removed peacefully. In anticipation of Chinese Premier Wen Jiabao's visit, Foreign Secretary Nirupama Rao has correctly stated on December 4, 2010 that 'we need an ambitious agenda for engagement'.

—14 December, 2010, The Pioneer

Need to Scrutinise India's Foreign Policy

The US cables put out by the WikiLeaks have not only established the fact that the US diplomats were keeping a vigil over every aspect of India's domestic politics and governance but also reveals how an anxious India sought US approval for a range of major decisions. It deserves to be stated that the Opposition parties have always warned the Congress-led UPA regime to maintain a distance from America so that the US Administration do not dictate or influence public policy decisions. However, the leaked US cables show that the Government headed by Prime Minister Manmohan Singh has consciously allowed itself to be manipulated by the US.

Responding to the Lok Sabha debate on March 23, 2011 Mr Singh questioned the authenticity of the cables by observing, "It was not possible for the Government to confirm the veracity or the contents of such communication." Mr Singh did not stop at dismissing the cables as unverified and unverifiable, he adopted a cavalier approach stating that "If they exist, they would be communications from the US diplomats stationed in New Delhi to their Government in Washington".

Although Mr Singh was being disingenuous by trying to describe the revelations as figments of imagination of a fertile mind, a few facts which have emerged from the cables clearly indicate that every event of consequence was under the scrutiny of American intelligence agencies in India. A look at some important facts that found mention in the US cables will substantiate the argument. First, a cable of April 6, 2005 reported by the Indian media on March 27, 2011, reveals that US Ambassador David Mulford described Congress president and UPA chairperson Sonia Gandhi as "pro-Communist" and that she appeared "more comfortable working with the often high-caste and well-educated Communists than regional satraps of the State based parties". This may have been the reason why US Secretary of State Hillary Clinton wanted Mr Montek Singh Ahluwalia and not Mr Pranab Mukherjee for the crucial Ministry of Finance as she wanted to checkmate Ms Gandhi's so-called cordial relations with Left parties. It is clear that the Cabinet-making process and the picking of Ministers were subjected to close scrutiny and America's preference for pro-American Ministers was publicly mentioned and conveyed.

Second, the foreign policy matters of India were not kept a secret to the Obama Administration. According to the New Delhi Embassy cable of May 1, 2009 and July 7, 2009 to the US State Department, India's newly appointed Permanent Representative to the UN, Mr Hardeep Puri, conveyed that "... the US-India bilateral relationship had benefited from a 'paradigm shift'" and India seeks "a greater degree of convergence" with the US on foreign policy. How can Mr Singh show innocence after these documented revelations?

The most sensational disclosure in the cable was the description of former representative to the UN Mr Nirupam Sen as "a dyed-in-the-wool Non-Aligned Movement advocate who made coordination with the Indians in the UN difficult". The US was happy with the selection of Mr Puri as he appeared "pragmatic". It implies that Mr Puri is a trustworthy diplomat for the Americans unlike Mr Sen. Again, the cables of March 15 and 17 clearly show that Americans were pulling all strings for playing a 'fraternal' role in India's foreign policy and had influenced India's attitude towards Iran and its decision on the Iran-Pakistan-India gas pipeline.

Further, Mr Singh's Cabinet was clearly tilted in favour of American arms and ammunitions industry. The Indian media reported on March 28, 2011 that the 'New Framework for the India-US Defence Relationship' signed in July 2005 promises extremely profitable business for the US as according to the US estimation, the Indian market for weapons import is worth "more than $27 billion" and it stands to gain from a "closer relationship and cooperation between India-America military establishment".

It is no secret that American corporates are lobbying extensively in India for the pursuit of their business goals and are trying to influence India's decision-making processes. India's Ambassador to the US informed the Government of India about bribes paid by American multinational companies to Indians, including public sector enterprises. Even Dow Chemical Company, the new avatar of Union Carbide—the company responsible for the Bhopal gas tragedy in 1984—is engaged in negotiations and networking with pliable politicians and bureaucrats of Maharashtra.

Therefore, how can one accept Mr Singh's contemptuous dismissal of the WikiLeaks cables in the light of such hard facts? Especially, when the increasing influence of America on Indian public policy formulation whether domestic or foreign is obvious.

Indians should be wary of the fact that the US-led NATO's armed forces have established a permanent headquarter in the neighbourhood. If the US can militarily intervene in Iraq, Afghanistan and Libya, with a view to impose a regime of their own choice and follows a policy of 'regime change' in countries of direct strategic and economic interests to India, it is imperative that we analyse the direct impact of US foreign policy on India.

—15 April, 2011, The Pioneer

New Strategic Realities Emerging in Asia

President Barack Obama's announcement of the withdrawal of troops from Afghanistan has clearly conveyed a global message—America's self-appropriated role as the sole 'super policeman' has proved costly and extremely counter-productive because nation's economy cannot carry the burden of fighting wars to protect its so-called national interests. Though Mr Obama has observed that "the tide of war is receding" but in blunt recognition of domestic economic strains, he frankly admits that "it's time to focus on nation-building at home".

It's not just the US that feels the heat of economic downturn at home, other European members of the NATO forces are also pulling out of war in Afghanistan as European economies too confront a 'stagnation of growth'. That apart, many crisis-ridden members of the European community are engaged in 'crisis management' on the basis of short-term and long-term 'bail out programmes'. Moreover, 20 years of American global 'hegemony' has taken a heavy toll on economic and socio-political fabric of the country. This could better explain the erosion in popular support for the war-mongering activities of the US Presidents from Mr George W Bush to Mr Obama.

Notwithstanding the alarming reality, the foreign policy-makers in India reposed full faith in the capacity of our 'strategic partner' on bilateral issues related to India-Pakistan and Indian-Afghanistan. But in the process they overlook the fact that the Pakistani Army—the real centre of power in the country—considers India its enemy number one and that it has not revised its military doctrine of directing all its energy against India. It shows that India has not learnt any lessons from the past relationship with Pakistan.

Yet India and Pakistan cannot turn their faces away from the compulsions of geographically determined status. The persistent 'trust-deficit' between these two neighbouring countries is the product of Pakistan's India-focussed strategic doctrine. In this context, it seems that India-Pakistan bilateral disputes were not enough to create disturbed situation in South Asia, a difficult new chapter of Afghanistan has opened new areas of conflict between India and Pakistan.

America's long war against Al Qaeda and Taliban for the last 10 years has completely shattered every structure of the Government in Afghanistan. A defeated and humiliated America and NATO armed forces are in disarray because popular opinion in their countries suffering from the impact of severe economic crisis are retreating in haste and leaving Afghan people to their own fate. The retreating Americans recognise this fact and General David Petraeus stated, that "More needs to be done, not only against those extremist elements that are threatening the security of Pakistan but also against those that are causing problems for neighbouring countries—Afghanistan foremost among them."

The real implication of American approach towards Afghanistan problem is that the armed forces need to be withdrawn 'gradually'. But at the same time, it looks that the US is in no mood to completely vacate the space occupied by it in Afghanistan because American security policy-makers are convinced that the presence of the forces in Afghanistan is essential for safeguarding strategic interests in Central Asia, South Asia and Russia. What Mr Obama has given from left hand, he has kept his military options in his right hand and its means NATO forces are permanently going to stay in this region.

The new strategic orientation of America in Afghanistan leaves India and Pakistan to fight their own battles because Pakistan wants 'strategic depth' in Afghanistan and India has its own stakes in Afghanistan which bring it in confrontation with Pakistan.

On the other hand, Afghanistan President Hamid Karzai may be feeling happy at the turn of events. But he must not forget that other warlords, Al Qaeda and Taliban, are not interested in keeping his Government in the saddle. And the Pakistani Army, with the support of Islamic militants both in its own country and in Afghanistan, is not going to leave easily the territorial boundaries of its very precious neighbour.

American and other interested parties want India to support nation-building and infrastructural development of Afghanistan. This is a very tall agenda for India to handle such an enormous task in unsettled conditions in Afghanistan. America is handing over the burden of reconstruction of wreaked economy without the protective umbrella of Americans who have to play an active role in Pakistan. In fact, the US cannot withdraw its forces without ensuring a guaranteed role for India.

Pakistan is an active player in Afghanistan irrespective of whether or not the Americans are engaged in Pakistan or vacating the military space in the region. The central issue is that India is bound to operate in hostile territory in Afghanistan because Pakistan has always considered Afghanistan as its zone of influence. It deserves to be mentioned that Mrs Indira Gandhi, considered as friend of Soviet Union, did not agree with Brezhnev–Kosygin interventionist policy in 1979 because as the Prime Minister of India she considered Afghanistan an Indian zone of influence. And much water has flown down the Ganges from 1979 to 2011 because Americans with the full support of Pakistan have given birth to Islamic fundamentalists like Al Qaeda, Taliban and other anti-India religious fanatic forces during their post-September 11, 2011 adventure in that area.

It is no secret that Pakistani agencies like the ISI have patronised and lionised the religious fanatics and allowed the anti-terrorist forces to operate openly against America and India. The American and Pakistani and Army and the ISI do not have any control over the Islamic religious zealots and India has been left to fight its own battles on its own. This is the situation at the ground level. The option before India and Pakistan is to resolve its own dispute on the basis of the available resources.

Recently concluded Foreign Secretaries-level meeting between these two countries in Pakistan has come to recognise that it has to fight against Islamic militants and if both these countries realise that terrorism is their common enemy, new steps in positive manner can be evolved.

—30 June, 2011, The Pioneer

UPA has Failed on Foreign Policy Front

Immersed in multiple scams at home, the Congress-led UPA Government has failed to deal with foreign policy challenges which are staring the nation in the face. It is a well known fact that foreign policy cannot be left hanging in the air but the politically weak and shaky Government of Prime Minister Manmohan Singh has failed give it appropriate time and attention.

During her visit to India for the second round of the India-US Strategic Dialogue, US Secretary of State Hillary Clinton pontificated that it's time India take on a leading role in the region. Ms Clinton also observed that much of 21st Century history will be written in Asia which, in turn, will be influenced by the strategic partnership between the US and India, and India's relationship with its neighbouring countries. Of course, her statement about India's role as a leader in the region has raised the hackles of the Pakistani leadership.

That apart, what is worth noticing, is that her visit to the subcontinent from July 18 to 20 coincided with two major crises hovering over the the Obama Administration: the debate over raising the US debt ceiling and the US's strained relationship with ally Pakistan. These reflect on the the US's declining strategic and economic supremacy. Moreover, its decision to withdraw forces from Afghanistan would also affect peace and security in the region.

Though Mr Singh warned Ms Clinton that US withdrawal from Afghanistan 'could hurt India', his comments went unnoticed. Yet, consequences of American withdrawal from Afghanistan are grave, since that would leave India and Pakistan to fight it out as they both seek to establish their own areas of influence in war-torn Afghanistan.

It is one thing to sermonize that India should continue to play positive role in the nation-building processes of Afghanistan, and another side of the reality is that Americans are leaving a divided and strife-ridden country where Pakistan is waiting to extend its control. Clearly, Ms Clinton had nothing to assure India, the US's most important strategic partner, either in the area of post-America withdrawal from Afghanistan or on nuclear trade except to reassert that Indian Nuclear Suppliers' Liability Act is inhibiting American firms to engage with India.

The real explanation for flatness of India-US talks from July 18-20 is crisis-ridden America is not in a position to provide global leadership and crisis-riddenUPA Government has no capacity to keep away Pakistan's interventionist strategies in Afghanistan. Not only this, the Hamid Karzai Government is also moving step by step towards disintegration an it will be a tragedy for South Asia if Afghanistan becomes a battleground among various tribes — the Talibans and other fundamentalist groups. Ms Clinton's visit to India and Pakistan did not yield any result and our weak Prime Minister could not reciprocate to Ms Clinton's rhetoric that 'India should lead' Asia.

The visitor from America and her Indian hosts were found quite inadequate in making appropriate foreign policy choices because both countries do not have political capabilities to fulfil their promises either on trade in the area of Nuclear supplies or laying down the foundations of appropriate framework for post-America withdrawal situation which will develop in Afghanistan.

While India-US Strategic Dialogue has not borne any fruits or broken any new path in foreign policy, the visit of Foreign Minister of Pakistan Hina Rabbani Khar has constructively resulted in establishing new confidence building measures. Indian foreign policy makers had very modest expectations from Ms Khar's visit and the talks have laid down the foundations for 'future dialogue' between the two neighbouring countries which have a great burden of history over their shoulders?

Ms Khar referred to 'history of hostilities', and asserted that 'new young generation of Pakistan aspires friendship with India'. Ms Khar expressed her desire for a new era of ties and stated, "The dialogue process should be uninterrupted and uninterruptable, keeping in building trust and be result oriented".

Foreign policy discussions between India and Pakistan on July 27 have been conducted in a very special context and situations facing both the countries. Indian Government from 2009 to 2011 has been compelled to 'engage' itself with domestic politically divisive issues, Pakistan is in trouble because its relationship with the US have deteriorated. It was revealed clearly when Americans withheld $800 million aid to its 'most important strategic ally'. And the American war on Afghanistan compelled it to accord the status of 'non-NATO ally' to Pakistan.

This new special status brought a lot of goodies to Pakistan from

America. Americans are clearly dissatisfied with 'anti-terrorism' operations taken by Pakistan especially on the eve of American withdrawal of military forces from Afghanistan.

—5 August, 2011, The Pioneer

Index